Turning Points

Communicating in English

Giuliano Iantorno

Mario Papa

ADDISON-WESLEY PUBLISHING COMPANY

Reading, Massachusetts • Menlo Park, California • New York
Don Mills, Ontario • Wokingham, England • Amsterdam
Bonn • Sydney • Singapore • Tokyo • Madrid • San Juan

A Publication of the World Language Division

Project Director: Ann Strunk   Developmental Editor: Talbot Hamlin

Editorial Staff
Jennifer Bixby, Claire Smith

Production/Manufacturing: James W. Gibbons

Consultants
Robert Saitz   Charles Skidmore

Design, production and illustration provided by Publishers' Graphics, Inc., Bethel, Connecticut. Artists: Leslie Dunlap, Ethel Gold, Pamela Johnson, Jane Kendall.

Cover design by Marshall Henrichs.

Photographs: Air Transportation Association of America, 28 d; AMTRAK, 28 g; The Bettmann Archive, Inc., 10 b, 112 d,f; Boston Symphony Orchestra, 14 g, 23 b; British Information Services, 10 g, 14 c; Angelo Carlino, 23 c; Chrysler Corporation, 10 e; Columbia Manufacturing Company, 28 b; Harley-Davidson Motor Company, Inc., 28 f; International Harvester Company, 28 e; Senator Edward M. Kennedy, 14 e; Metropolitan Transit Authority (New York City), 22 e, 28 a; Movie Star News, 10 a,d,f, 14 a,b, 24 b,e,h, 96 (both), 112 b,e, 120; National Aeronautical and Space Administration, 23 a, 112 c; New York Convention and Visitors Bureau, Inc., 22 a,b,c,d, 23 a,b,c, 81 (all), 88, 89 (all); Salem Evening News, 22 c; Star File, 10 c, 14 d,h, 112 g; United States Supreme Court, 14 f; Volkswagen of America, 28 c.

ISBN 0-201-06315-8
ISBN 0-201-52151-2 School Spec. Ed.
 IJKLMNOP-WC-99876543210

CONTENTS

HAPPY BIRTHDAY! 1

BILL: Oh! Hi, John!
Come in!
JOHN: Hi, Bill!
Happy birthday!
BILL: Thank you.
JOHN: Bill, this is Tim.
He's English.
BILL: Hi, Tim!
TIM: Hello, Bill!
Happy birthday!
JOHN: Here's a present for you.
BILL: Oh, thanks!
JOHN: You're welcome.

Communication Points
Introduce people and tell nationality

1. Guess! Mexican? American? English?

  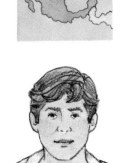 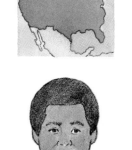

a. This is Tim.
   He's . . . .

b. This is Bill.
   He's . . . .

c. This is Pedro.
   He's . . . .

d. This is John.
   He's . . . .

2. Introduce these people to your partner.

Student A: . . . , this is Tim. He's English.
Student B: Hi, Tim.

3. Now introduce these people to your partner.

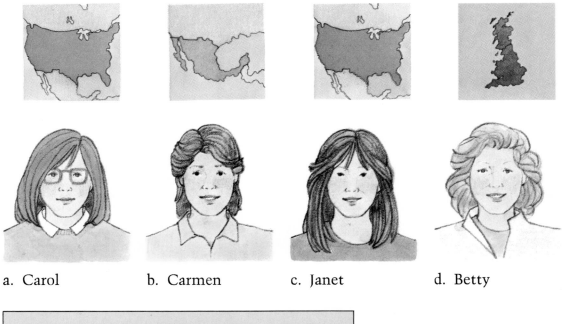

a. Carol

b. Carmen

c. Janet

d. Betty

Student A: . . . , this is Carol. She's American.
Student B: Hi, Carol.

Give and receive presents

Give four presents to your partner.

a. a book

b. a radio

c. a watch

d. a pen

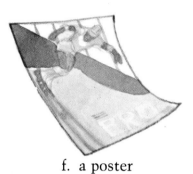

e. a football

f. a poster

> Student A: Here's a radio for you.
> Student B: Oh, thanks.
> Student A: You're welcome.

Language Points

Listening

What presents are they getting? Write on your paper.

Tim	?	?	?
John	?	?	?
Pedro	?	?	?

Sing a song!

HAPPY BIRTHDAY

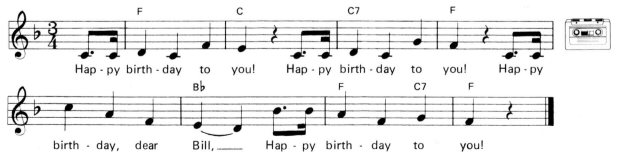

Hap-py birth-day to you! Hap-py birth-day to you! Hap-py

birth-day, dear Bill,____ Hap-py birth-day to you!

Role play

What are they saying? Practice with your partner.

a.

b.

c.

Practice Points

1. Write what you and your partner said in the role play.
2. Give these presents to your partner. Then write what you both said.

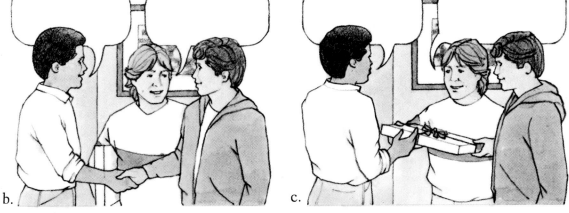

a. a cassette recorder   b. a record player   c. a camera   d. a TV   e. a radio

f. a watch   g. a pen   h. a football   i. a poster   j. a book

Check Points

Communication Points

Introduce people and tell nationality

Give and receive presents

Bill, this is Tim. He's English.

Here's a present for you.
Thank you. / Oh, thanks.

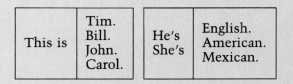

This is	Tim. Bill. John. Carol.	He's She's	English. American. Mexican.

Here's a	present radio book	for you.

Words and Expressions

a	English	is	present	this
American	football	Mexican	radio	TV
book	for	pen	record player	watch
camera	here's (here is)	poster	she's (she is)	you
cassette recorder	he's (he is)			

Come in.	Hello!	Oh, thanks.
Happy birthday!	Hi!	You're welcome.

2 WHERE ARE YOU FROM?

TIM: Hello, my name's Tim. What's your name?

CAROL: Carol. Where are you from, Tim?

TIM: I'm from London.

CAROL: London? Oh, you're English.

TIM: Yes, I am.

CAROL: Tim, this is Janet. She's from San Francisco.

TIM: Hello, Janet!

JANET: Hi!

Communication Points
Introduce yourself

A:	Hi! My name's . . . . What's your name?
B:	. . . .

Ask where people are from

A:	Where are you from?
B:	I'm from . . . .

Introduce people

a. Janet Koga is from San Francisco.

b. John Cooper is from New York.

c. Tim Bennett is from London.

d. Sue MacDuff is from Toronto.

e. Pedro Ramirez is from Mexico City.

f. Bill Day is from New York.

Introduce these people to your partner.

A:	. . . , this is Janet. She's from San Francisco.
B:	Hi, Janet.

A:	. . . , this is John. He's from New York.
B:	Hi, John.

Language Points
Open dialogue

 Talk to Carol.

CAROL: Hi! My name's Carol. What's your name?

YOU: . . . .

CAROL: Where are you from?

YOU: . . . .

CAROL: Oh, you are? This is Tim. He's English.

YOU: . . . .

TIM: Hello!

Practice Points

1. Write the "Open dialogue."

2. Use the chart below. Write six true sentences.

John Janet Pedro Tim Sue Bill	is from	London. Mexico City. New York. San Francisco. Toronto.	He She	is	American. Canadian. English. Mexican.

3. Read what the people say in picture a. Write dialogues for pictures b to e.

a. Sue   Carol

b. Tim   John

c. Janet   Bill

d. Pedro   John

e. You   Your partner

4. Who are they? Where are they from? Write the answers. The first two are done for you.

a. This is Michael Jackson.
    He is American.
    He is from Gary, Indiana.

b. This is Wayne Gretzky.
    He is Canadian.
    He is from Edmonton, Alberta.

c. This is Paul . . . .
    He is English.
    He is from Liverpool.

d. This is . . . .
    She is . . . .
    She is from Brooklyn.

e. This is . . . .
    He is . . . .
    He is from Mexico City.

f. This is . . . .
    She is . . . .
    She is from New York.

g. This is . . . .
    She is . . . .
    She is from . . . .

Check Points
Communication Points

Introduce yourself	Hi! My name's John.
	What's your name?
	My name's Tim.
Ask where people are from	Where are you from?
	I'm from New York.
Introduce people	Tim, this is Janet. She's from San Francisco.
	Hello, Janet!

My name's	Tim. John. Janet.	What's your name?

Where are you from?	I'm from London. He's from New York. She's from Tokyo.	Oh, you're	English. American. Japanese.

Words and Expressions

am	from	I'm (I am)	she	yes
are	he	my	what's (what is)	your
Canadian	I	name	where	you're (you are)

3 HOW DO YOU DO, MR. DAY?

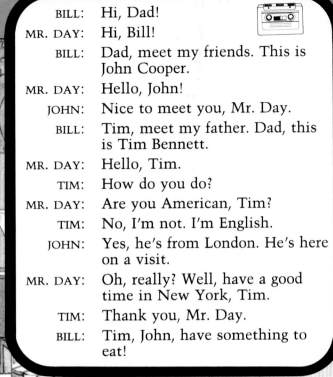

BILL: Hi, Dad!

MR. DAY: Hi, Bill!

BILL: Dad, meet my friends. This is John Cooper.

MR. DAY: Hello, John!

JOHN: Nice to meet you, Mr. Day.

BILL: Tim, meet my father. Dad, this is Tim Bennett.

MR. DAY: Hello, Tim.

TIM: How do you do?

MR. DAY: Are you American, Tim?

TIM: No, I'm not. I'm English.

JOHN: Yes, he's from London. He's here on a visit.

MR. DAY: Oh, really? Well, have a good time in New York, Tim.

TIM: Thank you, Mr. Day.

BILL: Tim, John, have something to eat!

Communication Points
Greet people

The Days

The Coopers

a.   Mrs. Day   Mr. Day
           Carol   Bill

b.   John   Mr. Cooper
        Mrs. Cooper

c.   Tim Bennett

d.   Miss Bennett

Introduce your partner to these people.

> A: Mr. Day, this is . . . .
> B: Nice to meet you, Mr. Day.

> A: Bill, this is . . . .
> B: Hello, Bill.

Find out a person's identity

Be one of the people on this page. Let your partner guess who you are.

> A: Are you American/English/Japanese, . . . ?
> B: Yes, I am/No, I'm not.
> A: Are you from Gary/London/Tokyo, . . . ?
> B: Yes, I am/No, I'm not.

a. NAME
Meryl Streep

NATIONALITY
American

CITY
Los Angeles

COUNTRY
United States

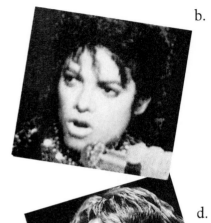

b. NAME
Michael Jackson

NATIONALITY
American

CITY
Gary

COUNTRY
United States

c. NAME
Princess Diana

NATIONALITY
English

CITY
London

COUNTRY
England

d. NAME
Paul McCartney

NATIONALITY
English

CITY
Liverpool

COUNTRY
England

e. NAME
Senator Kennedy

NATIONALITY
American

CITY
Boston

COUNTRY
United States

f. NAME
Justice Sandra Day
O'Connor

NATIONALITY
American

CITY
Washington, D.C.

COUNTRY
United States

g. NAME
Seiji Ozawa

NATIONALITY
Japanese

CITY
Tokyo

COUNTRY
Japan

h. NAME
Yoko Ono

NATIONALITY
Japanese

CITY
Osaka

COUNTRY
Japan

Locate places

1. Copy and complete.

a. London is
in England.

b. Boston is in the
United States.

c. Tokyo is
in . . . .

d. Los Angeles
is . . . .

e. Liverpool . . .
. . . .

f. . . .
. . . .

g. . . .
. . . .

h. . . .
. . . .

2. Make true and false statements like this:

> A: New York's in the United States.
> London's in Japan.
> B: True, New York's in the United States.
> False, London's in *England*.

Language Points
Listening

Listen to the dialogues. Write the nationality and city or town of each person. Make a chart like this.

Name	Nationality	City
Miss Bennett	? ? ?	? ? ?
Carmen	? ? ?	? ? ?
John Davis	? ? ?	? ? ?

Open dialogue

You are in New York for a visit. Talk to Mr. Day.

MR. DAY: Hi! My name's Jim Day.

YOU: . . . .

MR. DAY: Nice to meet you. Are you American?

YOU: . . . .

MR. DAY: Oh, really? Are you here on a visit?

YOU: . . . .

MR. DAY: Well, have a good time in New York.

YOU: . . . .

Sing a song!

HOW DO YOU DO?

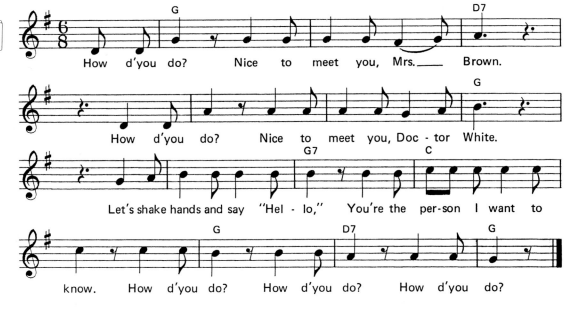

2nd Verse: How d'you do? Where are you from,
Mrs. Brown?
How d'you do? Where are you from,
Dr. White? *etc.*

Practice Points

1. Write the "Open dialogue."

2. Copy and complete these dialogues. Use *Hi, Hello,* or *Nice to meet you.*

a. JOHN: Dad, this is Bill Day.

   BILL: . . . , Mr. Cooper.

b. JOHN: Happy birthday, Bill.
              Meet my friend Tim.

   BILL: . . . , Tim.

c.   CAROL: . . . . My name's Carol Day.

        TIM: . . . , Carol. My name's Tim Bennett.

    CAROL: This is my mother.

  MRS. DAY: . . . , Tim.

        TIM: . . . , Mrs. Day.

    CAROL: And this is my father.

        TIM: . . . , Mr. Day.

3. Read the following dialogue.

English
Tim
Liverpool
London

YOU: Are you English, Tim?

TIM: Yes, I am.

YOU: Are you from Liverpool?

TIM: No, I'm not. I'm from London.

4. Now write dialogues for these people.

Mexican
Pedro
Monterrey
Mexico City

American
Janet
Los Angeles
San Francisco

Canadian
Sue
Montreal
Toronto

5. Look at the chart below and write six true sentences like this.

New York is in the United States.

London New York Monterrey Tokyo Montreal Mexico City Osaka Gary Toronto	United States Canada Mexico Japan England

Check Points

Communication Points

Greet people	Nice to meet you, Mr. Day. Hello, Bill.
Find out a person's identity	Are you American? No, I'm not. Are you from Tokyo? Yes, I am.
Locate places	London is in England. New York is in the United States.

Are you	American? English? Mexican?	Yes, I am. No, I'm not.	New York London Mexico City	is in	the United States. England. Mexico.

Words and Expressions

and	here	mother	not
city	in	Mr.	on
Dad	Japanese	Mrs.	the
father	meet	nationality	to
friends	Miss	no	visit

Have a good time!   Nice to meet you.   Oh, really?
How do you do?   Oh, I see.   Well, ...

HURRY UP, JOHN! 4

BILL: Good morning, Mrs. Cooper.

MRS. COOPER: Hi, Bill! Come in.

BILL: Is John here?

MRS. COOPER: Yes, he is. He's in his room. John!

JOHN: Yes, Mom.

MRS. COOPER: Bill's here.

BILL: Hurry up, John! We're late.

JOHN: We are? What time is it?

BILL: It's ten o'clock.

JOHN: Oh, gosh! . . . . I'm ready.

BILL: Well, let's go. Goodbye, Mrs. Cooper!

JOHN: Bye, Mom!

MRS. COOPER: Bye! Have a good time!

JOHN: Hey! Where's Carol?

BILL: Carol? She's with her friend Janet. They're at the bus stop. Let's go!

Communication Points

Count and add

1. Read these numbers.

1	**2**	**3**	**4**	**5**	**6**
one	two	three	four	five	six
7	**8**	**9**	**10**	**11**	**12**
seven	eight	nine	ten	eleven	twelve

2. Ask and answer with your partner.

1 + 1 = ?	3 + 4 = ?	4 + 1 = ?	7 + 2 = ?	6 + 2 = ?
6 + 4 = ?	10 + 2 = ?	3 + 3 = ?	2 + 1 = ?	5 + 3 = ?
4 + 7 = ?	2 + 2 = ?	4 + 2 = ?	3 + 1 = ?	6 + 1 = ?

> 2 + 3 = ?
> A: How much is two and three?
> B: Five.

Ask and tell time

1. Read these times.

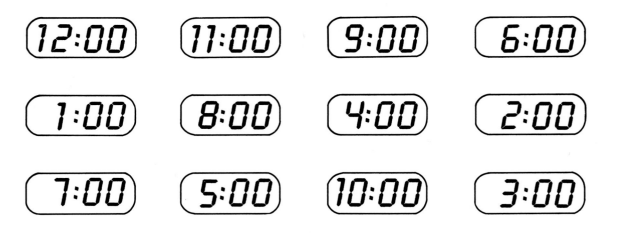

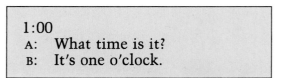

> 1:00
> A: What time is it?
> B: It's one o'clock.

2. Use the "Time Zone Map of the World" on page 21.

> A: It's one o'clock in Paris.
>   What time is it in New York?
> B: It's seven o'clock.

TIME ZONE MAP OF THE WORLD

| Mid-night | 1 am | 2 am | 3 am | 4 am | 5 am | 6 am | 7 am | 8 am | 9 am | 10 am | 11 am | Noon | 1 pm | 2 pm | 3 pm | 4 pm | 5 pm | 6 pm | 7 pm | 8 pm | 9 pm | 10 pm | 11 pm |

Arctic Ocean

9 am

Arctic Ocean

Fairbanks
2 am

10 pm 11 pm

5 am

4 pm

6 pm

9 pm

24 am

6 am

Moscow

5 pm

7 pm 8 pm

Quebec

Berlin

Peking

Phoenix Chicago 7 am New York Washington

London 1 pm Paris 3 pm

Ankara

Tokyo

Los Angeles

Houston

Madrid

Atlantic Ocean

Cairo

NOON

Pacific Ocean

Caracas

1 pm

Pacific Ocean

Lagos 3 pm

Singapore

Pacific Ocean

Lima 8 am 9 am

Indian Ocean

Rio de Janeiro

2 pm

8 pm 10 pm

Santiago

Capetown

Melbourne

International Dateline

Prime Meridian

| Standard Time Zones | Irregular Time | No Legal Time |

Ask names

a.   A: What's his name?
     B: Bill.

b.   A: What's her name?
     B: Carol.

c.

d.

e.

f.

g.

h.

Locate people

1. Ask your partner where these people are.

A: Where's John?
B: He's at the football game.

John   Mr. Wilde   Carol   Tim   Mrs. Cooper

at the
library

at the
zoo

at the
football game

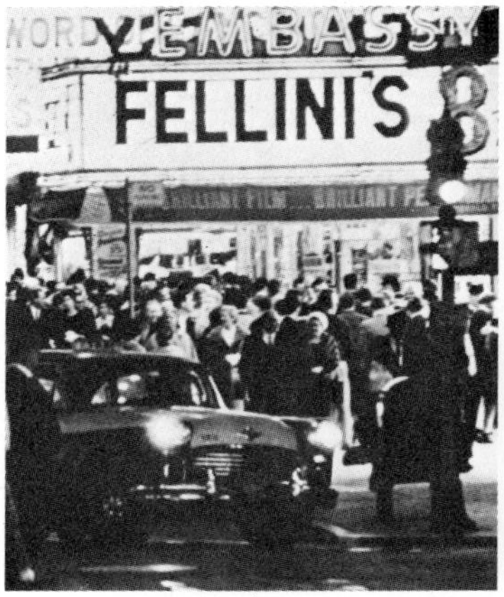

at the
movies

at the
bus stop

A: Where are Barbara and Sue?
B: They're at the movies.

Barbara and Sue   Tim and John

Carol and Janet   Mr. and Mrs. Cooper   Bill and Miguel

2. Make dialogues like this.

a. Sue/Barbara

b. John/Miguel

c. Bill/Tim

Language Points
Listening

Tell what you hear. Write the correct letter each time on your paper.

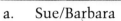

a. a rocket
   countdown

b. an orchestra
   conductor

c. a boxing
   match

Practice Points

1. Write the following times.

2:00 / It's two o'clock.

a. 2:00	b. 10:00	c. 9:00
d. 3:00	e. 8:00	f. 4:00
g. 7:00	h. 6:00	i. 11:00
j. 5:00	k. 12:00	l. 1:00

2. Copy and complete the sentences. Use *his* or *her*.

a. What's . . .
   name? Bill.

b. . . . name is
   The Incredible
   Hulk.

c. Carol is in . . .
   room.

d. . . . name is
   Stevie Wonder.

e. . . . name is
   Wonder
   Woman.

f. Where is John?
   He is in . . .
   room.

g. Where is Mrs.
   Cooper? She is
   with . . . friend.

h. What's . . .
   name? Liza
   Minnelli.

3. Look at the words in the box.

He's = He is.	They're = They are.
She's = She is	We're = We are.

**Now read the questions. Then copy and complete the answers.
Use *he's, she's, we're,* or *they're.***

a. Where are John and Bill?   . . . at the football game.
b. Where's John?   . . . in his room.
c. Where's Carol?   . . . with her friend.
d. Where are Carol and Janet?   . . . at the bus stop.
e. Tim, Bill, where are you?   . . . with John.
f. Where are Mr. and Mrs. Day?   . . . at the library.
g. Where are Tim and Bill?   . . . at the zoo.
h. Where's Janet?   . . . in her room.
i. Where's Tim?   . . . with his friend.
j. Carol, Janet, where are you?   . . . with Tim.

4. **Read the dialogues of Units 1 to 4. Write what people say when they meet. Write what they say when they leave.**
5. **Look at these pictures. What do these people say? Use the sentences in the box. Write on your paper.**

Good morning, Mrs. Cooper/ Hello, Bill/ Hi, John/ Bye/
Goodbye, Mrs. Day/ Bye, Mom/ Good morning, Mr. Day

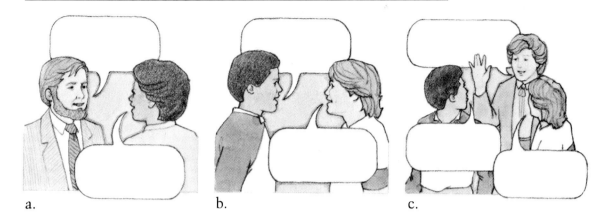

a.   b.   c.

Check Points

Communication Points

Count and add	How much is 2 and 3?
Ask and tell time	What time is it? It's one o'clock.
Ask names	What's his/her name?
Locate people	Where's John?/ He's at the football game. Where are Barbara and Sue?/ They're at the movies.

How much is	2 and 3? 3 and 5?

What's	his her	name?

Where's	John? Carol?
Where are	they? Barbara and Sue? you?

He She	is		
We They	are	at the	zoo.

He is He's	in	his	room.
She is She's		her	

| What time is it? | It's | one | o'clock. |
| | | two | |

Words and Expressions

			Number Names	
add	library	time	one	seven
at	movies	we	two	eight
bus stop	now	with	three	nine
football game	o'clock	zoo	four	ten
her	ready		five	eleven
his	room		six	twelve
it	they			

Bye!
Good morning.
Goodbye.
How much . . . ?

Hurry up!
Let's go.
Oh, gosh!
What time is it?

movies   cinema

Sing a song!

HONEY

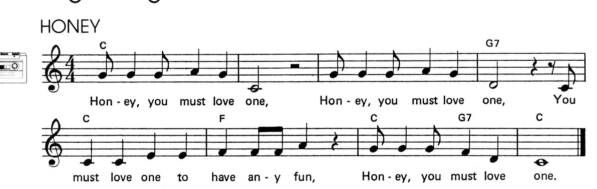

Hon - ey, you must love one, Hon - ey, you must love one, You must love one to have an-y fun, Hon - ey, you must love one.

2. Honey, you can't love two,
   Honey, you can't love two,
   You can't love two and still be true,
   Honey, you can't love two.

3. Honey, you can't love three, *etc.*
   You can't love three and get along
      with me, *etc.*

4. Honey, you can't love four, *etc.*
   You can't love four 'cause you'll
      want more, *etc.*

5. Honey, you can't love five, *etc.*
   You can't love five and take 'em for
      a drive, *etc.*

6. Honey, you can't love six, *etc.*
   You can't love six for you'll be in a fix, *etc.*

7. Honey, you can't love seven, *etc.*
   You can't love seven and still go to
      heaven, *etc.*

8. Honey, you can't love eight, *etc.*
   You can't love eight and keep 'em all
      straight, *etc.*

9. Honey, you can't love nine, *etc.*
   You can't love nine and still be mine, *etc.*

10. Honey, you can't love ten, *etc.*
    If you love ten you'll have to sing it all
       again, *etc.*

AN ENGLISH CAR 5

BILL:	Look, John! There they are. Tim's there, too. Carol! Tim!
CAROL:	Oh. You're here at last! Late as usual!
JOHN:	Yes, but we aren't late for the bus.
BILL:	John, look at that blue car!
JOHN:	Wow! It's big! Is it American?
BILL:	I don't know. Let's go look at it. It's a Bentley.
TIM:	A Bentley? That's an English car!
CAROL:	Hey, you guys! Here's our bus!

Communication Points

Identify vehicles

Ask your partner about the pictures.

a. a bus b. a bike c. a car d. an airplane

e. a truck f. a motorcycle g. a train

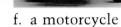

A:	What's picture *a*?
B:	It's a bus.

Locate people and things

HERE OR THERE?

> It's here.

> It's there.

Write *here* and *there* on your paper. With your partner, write the names of six things under *here* and six different things under *there*. Then ask and answer questions like these:

A:	Where's the car?
B:	It's here.

B:	Where's the bike?
A:	It's over there.

Write the names of people and places on your lists. Ask and answer questions like these. Explain why you say *here* or *there*.

> Where's Tim?

> He's **here** at the bus stop.

> Where's Tim?

> He's **there** at the bus stop.

Identify vehicles and colors

red   blue   yellow   white   black   brown   pink   green   orange

1. Talk to your partner.

> A: Look at that blue car!
> B: That's an American car.

a. an American car

b. an English bus

c. an Italian bike

d. a Japanese motor- cycle

e. an American train

2. Look at the pictures. Copy and complete the sentences. Explain.

a. The car is red.

b. The train is . . . .

c. The airplane is . . . .

d. The bus is . . . .

e. The truck is . . . .

f. The motorcycle is . . . .

3. Ask and answer questions about the pictures.

> A: What color is this car?
> B: It's red.

Describe vehicles

John and Tim are at the International Car Show. John is describing the cars. Take John's role and describe the cars to your partner.

> This big car is German. It's a Mercedes.
> That small car is Italian. It's a Fiat.

Ask about nationality

Ask your partner the questions. Then change roles.

Questions			Answers		
Am	I				you are.
Is	a Ferrari a Lincoln a Toyota a Bentley Tim Carol Pedro Sue John	Mexican? Italian? Japanese? American? English? Canadian?	Yes,		it is. he is. she is. they are.
Are	Mr. and Mrs. Cooper Mr. and Mrs. Bennett Mr. and Mrs. Fernandez		No,		you aren't. it isn't. he isn't. she isn't. they aren't.

Language Points

Guided dialogue

1. Copy and complete this dialogue. Use the sentences on the right, but put them in the correct order.

JOHN: . . . .
MRS. DAY: Hello, John. Come in.
JOHN: . . . .
MIGUEL: How do you do, Mrs. Day.
MRS. DAY: Hello, Miguel.
JOHN: . . . .
MRS. DAY: No, he isn't.
He's at the football game.
JOHN: . . . .
MRS. DAY: It's 11 o'clock.
JOHN: . . . .
MRS. DAY: Bye, John, bye, Miguel.

> JOHN:
> —Is Bill in?
> —Mrs. Day, this is Miguel.
> —11 o'clock?
> Oh, we're late!
> Goodbye, Mrs. Day
> —Good morning, Mrs. Day.
> —At the football game? What time is it, please, Mrs. Day?

2. Now practice the dialogue with your partner.

3. What does Bill say when John and Miguel get to the football game? Write a dialogue between Bill and John. Practice it with your partner.

Guessing game

Ask your partner to think of a car at the International Car Show.
Guess your partner's car. Use questions like these. Then change roles.

A:	Is it a big car?	A:	Is it Italian?
B:	Yes, it is.	B:	Yes, it is.
A:	Is it red?	A:	It's a Ferrari!
B:	Yes, it is.	B:	Yes, that's right.

Practice Points

1. **Copy these words or groups of words on your paper and write *a* or *an* before them.**

train	truck	Japanese car
book	American train	Mexican song
Italian car	poster	
airplane	English radio	

2. **Copy and complete the sentences. Use *am*, *is*, or *are*. Explain.**

a. . . . Tim English? Yes, he is.

b. . . . Carol and Janet Italian? No, they aren't.

c. . . . Sue Canadian? Yes, she is.

d. . . . I late? No, you aren't.

e. . . . a Ferrari an Italian car? Yes, it is.

f. . . . John American? Yes, he is.

g. . . . Mr. and Mrs. Cooper English? No, they aren't.

h. . . . Janet from San Francisco? Yes, she is.

3. **Write descriptions of the cars at the International Car Show.**

A Cadillac is an American car. It is big and blue.

4. **Look at these examples:**

John/room	Where's John? He's in his room.
Bill and Tim/movies	Where are Bill and Tim? They're at the movies.

Now do the same thing with these.

a. Tim/football game

b. Mr. and Mrs. Cooper/movies

c. Janet/zoo

d. Carol and Tim/bus stop

e. Barbara/library

f. Mr. Day/post office

g. Bill/his room

h. Miss Bennett/post office

i. Mrs. Day and Sue/bus stop

j. Miguel/football game

5. Look at these examples:

Tim/English/London/3/his room

Tim is English. He is from London. It is 3 o'clock and he is in his room now.

John and Bill/American/New York/8/the movies

John and Bill are American. They are from New York. It is 8 o'clock and they are at the movies now.

Now do the same thing with these.

a. Janet and Patricia/American/San Francisco/4/library
b. Pedro/Mexican/Mexico City/11/his room
c. Carol/American/New York/9/post office
d. Mr. and Mrs. Day/American/Baltimore/10/zoo
e. Miss Bennett/English/Liverpool/6/movies
f. Sue/Canadian/Toronto/5/her room
g. Mr. and Mrs. Cooper/American/Washington/1/bus stop
h. Miguel/American/San Antonio/3/football game
i. Toshi Kitano/Japanese/Osaka/12/his room
j. Mr. and Mrs. Bennett/English/London/7/zoo

Check Points
Communication Points

Identify vehicles and colors	What's picture a? It's a bus. Look at that blue car! That's an English car. What color is this car? It's red. Is it red/big/American?
Locate people and things	Where's Tim? He's over there, at the bus stop. Where's the car? It's here.
Describe vehicles	This big car is American. It's a Lincoln. That small car is Italian. It's a Fiat.
Ask about nationality	Is Pedro Mexican? Are Mr. and Mrs. Cooper American?

What's picture	a? b? c?	It's a	bus. car. etc.

Where's	Tim? Carol?	He's She's It's	here. over there.
Where are	Barbara and Sue? Mr. and Mrs. Day?	They're	

Look at that	blue red black	car.

That's	an	American English	bike. car.
	a	Japanese German	

The	car train	is	red. blue.

What color is this	car? bike?

It's	red. blue.

This That	small big	car bike	is	American. English. Japanese.

It's a	Lincoln. Bentley. Toyota.

Am	I		late? American? English? Mexican? Japanese? German?
Is	he she it John Carol		
Are	Mr. and Mrs. Cooper they		

Yes,	you are. he is. she is. it is. they are.
No,	you aren't. he isn't. she isn't. it isn't. they aren't.

Words and Expressions

			Color Names	
airplane	color	small	black	pink
an	German	that	blue	red
big	Italian	there	brown	white
bike	late	train	green	yellow
bus	look	truck	orange	
but	motorcycle			
car	our			

as usual	Let's go look at it.
At last!	over there
Hey, you guys!	That's right.
I don't know.	Wow!

motorcycle	motorbike
airplane	aeroplane
color	colour

MIGUEL:	Hey, can I play?
JOHN:	No, you can't. You're too young.
MIGUEL:	No, I'm not!
JOHN:	How old are you?
MIGUEL:	I'm twelve. I'm not too young to play with you.
JOHN:	All right. You can be the right fielder.
MIGUEL:	Okay.
JOHN:	Miguel, you're up! It's your turn to bat.
BILL:	Strike one!
JANET:	Oh, no!
JOHN:	Keep your eye on the ball, Miguel!
BILL:	Strike two!
JANET:	Strike two! Oh, no!
(Voices):	He's going to strike out! No! He hit it! Look at him go!
JOHN:	It's a home run! Miguel, you're great!

Communication Points
Count and add

1. Read these numbers.

13 thirteen	16 sixteen	19 nineteen	22 twenty-two
14 fourteen	17 seventeen	20 twenty	23 twenty-three
15 fifteen	18 eighteen	21 twenty-one	

2. Add these numbers.

$8 + 7 = ?$ $9 + 8 = ?$ $11 + 9 = ?$ $10 + 6 = ?$

$10 + 11 = ?$ $6 + 12 = ?$ $9 + 5 = ?$ $14 + 6 = ?$

$15 + 2 = ?$ A: How much is fifteen and two?
B: Seventeen.

Ask and tell ages

A: I'm fourteen. How old are you?
B: I'm fifteen.

Ask and tell name/age/city

A: What's his name?
B: Tim.

A: How old is he?
B: He's fifteen.

A: Where's he from?
B: He's from London.

Tim—15
London

a. John—14
New York

b. Janet—13
San Francisco

c. Sue—19
Toronto

d. Pedro—18
Mexico City

Give information

1. Copy the questions. Choose and write correct answers.

a. Is Tim English?
Yes, he is.
No, he isn't.

b. Is this car
American?
Yes, it is.
No, it isn't.

c. Are Mr. and Mrs.
Cooper at the
post office?
Yes, they are.
No, they aren't.

d. Is Pedro at the
library?
Yes, he is.
No, he isn't.

e. Is Carol American?
Yes, she is.
No, she isn't.

f. Is Bill English?
Yes, he is.
No, he isn't.

g. Is the Ferrari Italian?
Yes, it is.
No, it isn't.

h. Is Sue Mexican?
Yes, she is.
No, she isn't.

i. Are John and Tim at the
football game?
Yes, they are.
No, they aren't.

2. Ask and answer the questions with your partner.

A: Is Tim English?
B: Yes, he is.

Ask for permission

Ask your partner's permission to do these things.

play with you	have something to drink	read this book
be right fielder	listen to the radio	have that poster
hit the ball	go to the zoo	go to the movies with you

> A: Can I play with you?
> B: Yes, you can/No, you can't.

Language Points

Listening

Listen to the radio program *Twenty Questions*. Write the ages of Mark, Kim, Mario, and Jane and the towns where they live. Make a chart like this.

	Age	Town
Mark Spencer	???	???
Kim Wang	???	???
Mario Garcia	???	???
Jane Spokowski	???	???

Look and find out

Look at the birthday cakes. How old is each person?

Robert

Elizabeth

Anne

José

> A: How old is Robert?
> B: He's . . . .
>
> A: How old is Anne?
> B: She's . . . .

Reading

BASEBALL DIAMOND

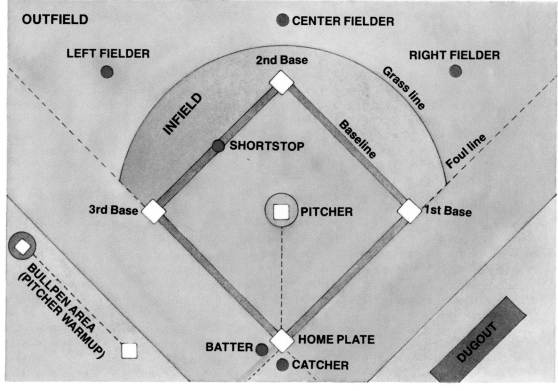

BASEBALL

American baseball is an exciting sport, and lots of people in the United States play it.

Elementary schools, high schools, and colleges have baseball teams, and, of course, there are professional teams.

Some famous professional teams are the New York Yankees, the Houston Astros, the Los Angeles Dodgers, the Boston Red Sox, and the Baltimore Orioles.

In the fall, the best professional teams play in the World Series. Fans cheer for their favorite teams. Millions of people watch the games on television or listen to them on the radio.

There are nine players on each side in a baseball game. They play on a field called a "diamond." The pitcher on one team throws the ball, and a batter on the other team tries to hit it with a bat. Everyone is excited when the batter hits a home run.

Many boys and girls and men and women play baseball. There are "Little Leagues" for children, but many people make up their own teams each time they play.

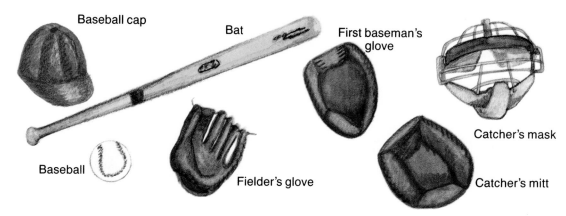

Write the word that goes with each picture. Use these words:

fans   diamond   pitcher

team   home run   batter

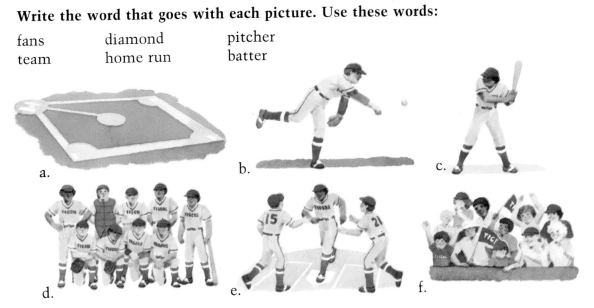

a.   b.   c.

d.   e.   f.

Practice Points

1. Write sentences about these people.

Name: Carol	*Her name is Carol, and she is thirteen. Carol is from New York.*
Age: 13	
City: New York	

a. Name: Bill
   Age: 14
   City: New York

d. Name: Janet
   Age: 13
   City: San Francisco

b. Name: Tim
   Age: 15
   City: London

e. Name: Sue
   Age: 19
   City: Toronto

c. Name: Pedro
   Age: 18
   City: Mexico City

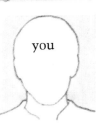

you

f. Name: . . .
   Age: . . .
   City . . .

2. Copy and complete.

a. Bill is from New York, so he is American.
b. Sue is from Toronto, so she is . . . .
c. Pedro is from Mexico City, so . . . .
d. Janet . . . .
e. Tim . . . .
f. I . . . .

3. Make sentences with these words. Then match each sentence with a picture.

a. out./going/strike/to/He's
b. run./a/home/It's
c. car./an/That's/English
d. big/The/car./is/Ferrari/a/Italian
e. that/truck?/is/Where/black
f. Japanese/is/The/motorcycle./small/a/Honda

1.
2.
3.
4.
5.
6.

4. Look at "Ask for permission" on page 38. Write ten questions and answers.

Can I go to the movies with you?
Yes, you can.
No, you can't.

5. Copy the following questions and write short answers.

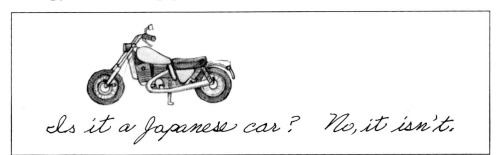

Is it a Japanese car?   No, it isn't.

a. Are Janet and Carol at the post office?

d. Is Sue from Toronto?

b. Is Bill at the zoo?

e. Are Tim and Miguel at the movies?

c. Is Janet at the bus stop?

f. Is Carlos thirteen?

Check Points

Communication Points

Count and add	How much is 15 and 2? It's 17.
Ask and tell ages	How old are you? I'm twelve.
Ask and tell name/age/city	What's his/her name? Where's he/she from?
Give information	Is Tim English? Yes, he is./No, he isn't.
Ask for permission	Can I play with you? Yes, you can./No, you can't.

How much is	12 13	and	1? 2?

It's	13. 14. 15.

How old	are	you?
	is	he? she?

I'm He's She's	12. 14.

Is	he she it Tim	American? at the library?
Are	they Mr. and Mrs. Cooper	

Yes,	he she it	is.
	they are.	
No,	he she it	isn't.
	they aren't.	

Can I	play? read? write?

Yes, No,	you can. you can't.

What's	his her	name?

Words and Expressions

				Number Names	
ball	can't	have	read	thirteen	nineteen
baseball	diamond	hit	something	fourteen	twenty
bat	drink	home run	team	fifteen	twenty-one
batter	fans	listen	throw	sixteen	twenty-two
be	go	play	up	seventeen	twenty-three
can	great	post office	young	eighteen	

All right.	Keep your eye on the ball.	strike out
How old are you?	Look at him go!	You're up!
I'm not too young . . .	Okay.	

7 A GUITAR COURSE

Barbara is a friend of Janet's sister Patricia. Barbara is 19. She's a student at Bronx Community College in New York. She wants to take guitar lessons at the college.

BARBARA: Good morning! I'm here for the guitar lessons.

PETER: Oh, sure. What's your name, please.

BARBARA: Barbara Cruz.

PETER: Excuse me, what's your last name again?

BARBARA: Cruz—C-R-U-Z.

PETER: Okay. Now, what's your address?

BARBARA: 11 College Road, Riverdale.

PETER: 11 College Road, Riverdale. Now, your telephone number?

BARBARA: My phone number? It's 616-2280.

PETER: 616-2280, right. Are you a student here?

BARBARA: Yes. Here's my student I.D.

PETER: Okay.

BARBARA: What time is the first lesson?

PETER: Tomorrow at four-thirty in room 22.

BARBARA: Tomorrow at four-thirty. All right. Thanks.

Communication Points
Count from 20 to 99

Read these numbers.

20 twenty	**27** twenty-seven	**30** thirty
21 twenty-one	**28** twenty-eight	**40** forty
22 twenty-two	**29** twenty-nine	**50** fifty
23 twenty-three		**60** sixty
24 twenty-four		**70** seventy
25 twenty-five		**80** eighty
26 twenty-six		**90** ninety

50	20	30	80	90	70	40	24	60
94	45	70	57	21	69	99	33	82
83	71	95	60	96	34	58	46	22

Say telephone numbers

1. **Read aloud the numbers on the two telephones and the numbers in Tim's phone book. The figure 0 is pronounced either *oh* or *zero*.**

2. Ask your partner's telephone number.

> A: What's your telephone number?
> B: It's . . . .

Identify people

1. Read this dialogue with your partner.

MAN:	What's your name?
BARBARA:	Barbara Cruz.
MAN:	And your address?
BARBARA:	11 College Road, Riverdale.
MAN:	What's your phone number?
BARBARA:	616-2280.

STUDENT IDENTIFICATION CARD

Barbara Cruz

11 College Road

Riverdale, N.Y. 10463

(212) 616-2280

2. Make dialogues for each of these people. Take turns playing the roles.

a.

NEW YORK DRIVERS LICENSE

Miss Mary Bennett
NAME
28 Jones Street
ADDRESS
New York, New York 10014

(212) 919-2365
PHONE NO.

b.

Riverdale Public Library NO. **46531**

Name   Carlos Luis Ramos

Address 10 West Street

Riverdale, N.Y. 10471

Telephone (212) 616-7296

c.

AIR WORLD
NAME   Bill Day
ADDRESS   98 Hicks Street
CITY   Brooklyn Heights
STATE   New York, 11201
PHONE   217-4456

d.

PHOTOGRAPHIC IMAGES FOR BUSINESS AND INDUSTRY

Light Write

WALTER COOPER
35 E. 83 STREET
NEW YORK, NEW YORK 10028
PHONE: (212) 113-5783

Ask and say the time

A: What time is it?
B: It's . . . .

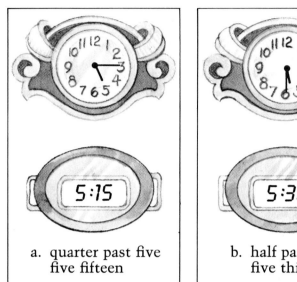

5:15	5:30	5:45

a. quarter past five
   five fifteen

b. half past five
   five thirty

c. quarter to six
   five forty-five

Take turns and say the time. Use both ways.

A: Is it half past twelve?
B: Yes, it's twelve thirty.

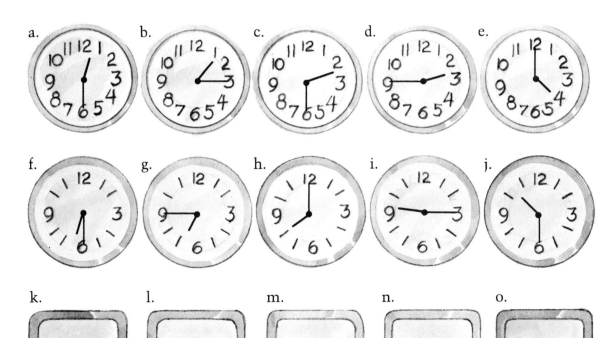

a.   b.   c.   d.   e.

f.   g.   h.   i.   j.

k.   l.   m.   n.   o.

11:00	11:15	12:00	12:45	1:30

Ask and tell when things happen

Look at the schedule. Then ask and answer with your partner.

School Activities
2:30 Camera club meeting
2:45 English club meeting
3:00 Model airplane club meeting
3:00 Baseball game
3:15 Art club meeting
3:30 Computer club meeting
3:45 School newspaper meeting
4:00 Radio club meeting
4:15 Chess club meeting
4:15 Science club meeting
4:45 Record club concert
7:30 Basketball game
8:00 School play

> A: What time is the camera club meeting?
> B: It's at 2:30.

Language Points

Listening

 Make a card like this on your paper. Then listen to the conversation and fill in the card for the person you hear.

BRONX COMMUNITY COLLEGE
Registration Card

Last Name _____ First Name _____

Address/Street _____ City _____ Zip _____

Telephone Number _____ Occupation _____

Course _____

Reading

Read this story. Then copy the identification card and fill it in.

A YOUNG JOURNALIST

Carlos Ramos is a young Mexican American. He is 22 years old and is Barbara's boy friend. Carlos is from Acapulco, but now he lives in New York with his family. They live at 10 West Street in Riverdale, near Barbara's house.

Many people come from other countries to live and work in New York. It is a big, exciting city and offers many opportunities.

Carlos is an American citizen now. He is a reporter at the *Evening Gazette,* a newspaper in New York. He plays the guitar and likes to sing Mexican and American songs.

(Name) _____

(Street Address) _____

(City) _____

(Age) _____

Practice Points

1. **Write these numbers on small pieces of paper. Mix the pieces of paper up. Then read them to your partner and let your partner write the numbers as you read them. Mix the numbers up again and reverse roles.**

A:	(says)	six
B:	(writes)	**6**

   6 32 55 44 13 90 30 80 14 36 70 15 60 12 8 29 99 19

2. **Write the following numbers in words.**

   21 30 32 40 43 50 54 60 65 70 76 87 90 98 99

   20 *twenty*

   35 *thirty-five*

3. **Write the following telephone numbers in words.**

   112-2340   147-9176   918-3327   561-4366

   215-5360 =   *two-one-five-five-three-six-zero*

4. Write the times.

It's quarter to six.

a.   b.   c.   d.   e.   f.

5. Read the schedule of school activities on page 48 and write the times of five activities. Use complete sentences.

The baseball game is at three o'clock.

Check Points

Communication Points

Count from 20 to 99

Say telephone numbers   What's your telephone number?
616-2280.

Identify people   What's your name?
Barbara Cruz.
What's your address?
11 College Road.

Ask and say the time   What time is it?
It's half past five.

Ask and tell when things happen   What time is the baseball game?
It's at 10:30.

What time is it?				

It's half past	seven. eight. nine.	It's	seven eight nine	thirty.

It's quarter	past	seven. eight.	It's	seven eight	fifteen.
	to	nine.		nine	forty-five.

Words and Expressions

				Number Names	
address	guitar	past	science	thirty	seventy
again	half	phone number	street	forty	eighty
art	last name	quarter	student	fifty	ninety
basketball	lesson	record	telephone	sixty	
card	meeting	road	tomorrow		
club	newspaper	school			

Excuse me.
Oh, sure.
please

3:30   half-four

ON THE PHONE

MRS. DAY:	Hello.
TIM:	Hello, Mrs. Day. This is Tim.
MRS. DAY:	Hi, Tim! How are you?
TIM:	Fine, thanks. And you?
MRS. DAY:	Fine.
TIM:	Is Bill home?
MRS. DAY:	Yes, he is.
TIM:	Can I speak to him, please?
MRS. DAY:	Sure. Hold on a minute.
BILL:	Hi, Tim! Where are you?
TIM:	I'm in a phone booth on Montague Street.
BILL:	Where?
TIM:	Montague Street.
BILL:	How do you spell it?
TIM:	M-O-N-T-A-G-U-E. It's near Court Street. The subway station, I mean.
BILL:	Oh, Montague Street. Sure. What time is it now?
TIM:	It's three o'clock.
BILL:	See you at the subway station at ten past three, then.
TIM:	Okay. So long.

Communication Points
Greet and respond to greetings

1. Practice the two dialogues below with your partner.

2. Play the roles of Mr. Cooper/Mrs. Cooper and John/Carol. Take turns. Use the expressions below.

A:	Hello, ...	How are you?
	Good morning, ...	

B:	Fine,	thanks.	And you?
	Okay,		
	Very well,	thank you.	And how are you?

A:	Fine,	thanks.
	Okay,	
	I'm very well,	thank you.

Talk on the phone

1. Practice the dialogues with your partner.

CAROL: Hello.

TIM: Hello, Carol. This is Tim.

CAROL: Hello, Tim.

TIM: Is Bill at home?

CAROL: Yes, he is.

TIM: Can I speak to him, please?

CAROL: Sure. Hold on a minute.

JANET: Hello.

BARBARA: Hello, Janet. This is Barbara.

JANET: Hello, Barbara.

BARBARA: Is Patricia at home?

JANET: Yes, she is.

BARBARA: Can I speak to her, please?

JANET: Sure. Hold on a minute.

2. Now play the roles of the people in the pictures.

Listen and say the alphabet

A B C D E F G

H I J K L M N O P

Q R S T U V W X Y Z

Practice reading the following groups of letters. Pay attention to the sounds in the different groups.

B	C	D	E	G	P	T	V	Z

F	L	M	N	S	X

A	H	J	K

I	Y

O

R

Sing a song!

ABC

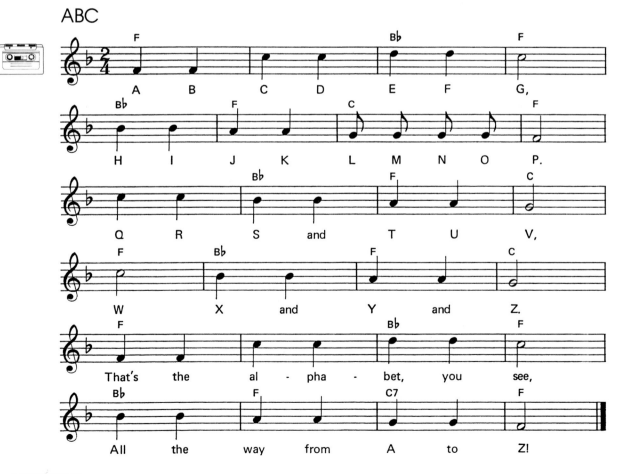

54   UNIT EIGHT

Spell street names

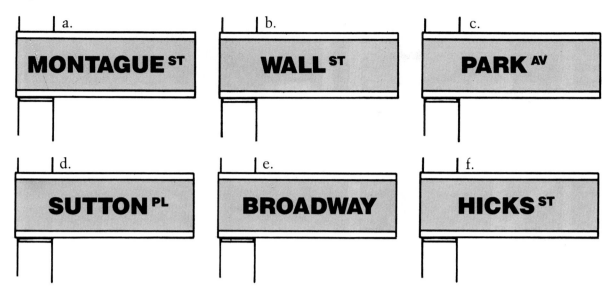

a. **MONTAGUE** ST
b. **WALL** ST
c. **PARK** AV
d. **SUTTON** PL
e. **BROADWAY**
f. **HICKS** ST

Spell your last name

Spell your last name. Take turns with your partner.

> A: What's your last name?
> B: ....
> A: How do you spell it?
> B: ....

Ask and say the time

1. Ask and answer with your partner.

> A: What time is it?
> B: It's ....

a. five past three
   three-oh-five

b. ten past three
   three ten

c. twenty past three
   three twenty

d. twenty-five past three
   three twenty-five

e. twenty-five to four
   three thirty-five

f. twenty to four
   three forty

g. ten to four
   three fifty

h. five to four
   three fifty-five

2. Draw eight clocks with different times. Ask your partner the time.

Arrange to meet people

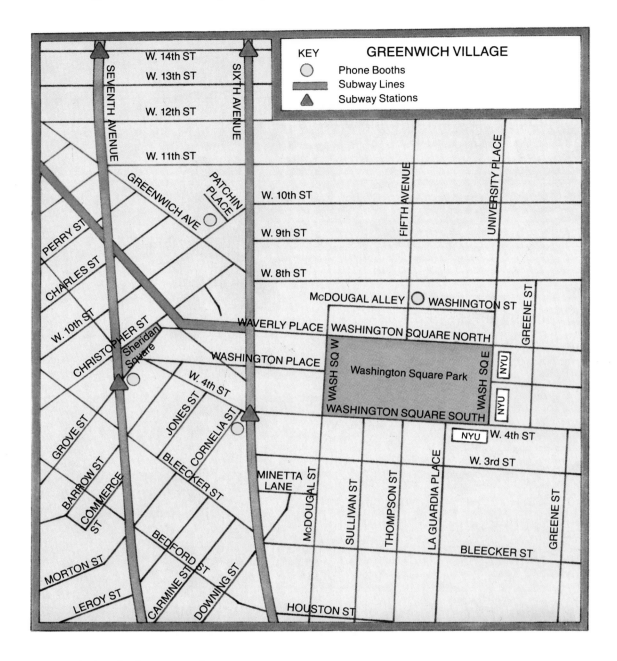

1. Read the dialogue with your partner.

BILL: Where are you, Tim?

TIM: I'm in a phone booth on Grove Street.

BILL: Grove Street? Where is it?

TIM: It's near the Sheridan Square subway station.

BILL: Oh, sure. What time is it now?

TIM: It's three o'clock.

BILL: See you at the subway station at ten past three, then.

2. Practice the dialogue again. Imagine you are in another phone booth on the map. Make the necessary changes. Then change roles.

Language Points
Listening

1. Listen to the recording. Bill and Carol are spelling some words. Write the words as you hear them.

2. Look at the words you have written. Draw lines around word number 2, word number 4, word number 8, and word number 12. Use these words to make an expression you often use when you meet a person for the first time.

Practice Points

1. Write dialogues like this one. Follow the punctuation in the example. You want to speak to Barbara, Carlos, Janet, and Tim.

> A: Is Bill at home?
> B: Yes, he is.
> A: Can I speak to him, please?

2. Write sentences like the example.

 *See you at the post office at ten past four.*

post office

a. Bill's house

b. bus stop

c. library

d. baseball game

e. zoo

f. football field

g. car show

h. movies

3. Call Bill. Arrange to meet to go to a football game. Write the conversation.

CAROL:	. . . . (Answers the phone.)
YOU:	. . . . (Greet. Say your name.)
CAROL:	. . . . (Responds.)
YOU:	. . . . (Ask to talk to Bill.)
CAROL:	. . . . (Responds.)
BILL:	. . . . (Greets.)
YOU:	. . . . (Ask if Bill is ready.)
BILL:	. . . . (Asks what time the game is.)
YOU:	. . . . (Say the time.)
BILL:	. . . . (Asks the time now.)
YOU:	. . . . (Say the time now: 2:30.)
BILL:	. . . . (Asks where you are.)
YOU:	. . . . (Say you are in a phone booth on . . . Street.)
BILL:	. . . . (Asks where it is.)
YOU:	. . . . (Say it is near the football field.)
BILL:	. . . . (Arranges to see you at the field at quarter to three.)
YOU:	. . . . (Say okay; end the conversation.)

Check Points

Communication Points

Greet and respond to greetings	Hello, Carol!/Good morning, Mr. Day. How are you? Fine, thanks./Okay. And you?/ Very well, thank you. And how are you? Fine/Okay.
Talk on the phone	Hello. Hello, Carol. This is Tim. Is Bill at home? Yes, he is. Can I speak to him, please?
Listen and say the alphabet	ABC . . .
Spell street names	M-O-N-T-A-G-U-E
Spell your last name	D-A-Y
Ask and say the time	What time is it? It's twenty past three. It's three twenty.
Arrange to meet people	See you at the football field at ten past three.

Where is it?	It's near	the subway station.

Can I speak to	him? her?

What time is it?

It's	five ten twenty twenty-five	to past	three.
	three	oh-five. ten. twenty. twenty-five.	

Words and Expressions

alphabet	him	phone booth	subway station	Hold on a minute.	See you . . .
fine	home	speak	very	How are you?	So long.
football field	near	spell	well		

football field	sports ground
subway	tube, underground
two-two-one-one	double two double one
phone booth	phone box

Sing a song!

BINGO

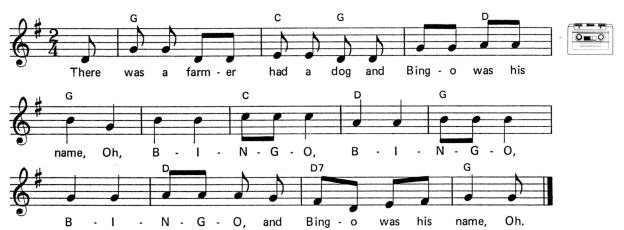

There was a farm-er had a dog and Bing-o was his
name, Oh, B - I - N - G - O, B - I - N - G - O,
B - I - N - G - O, and Bing-o was his name, Oh.

9 GRILLED CHEESE SANDWICHES

JOHN:	Hello, Miss Bennett.
MISS BENNETT:	Hi, John! How are you?
JOHN:	Fine, thanks.
TIM:	John!
JOHN:	Yes, Tim.
TIM:	I'm in the kitchen. Come on in!
JOHN:	Where?
TIM:	Here, in the kitchen. I'm making grilled cheese sandwiches. Have one.
JOHN	Oh, thanks! I'm hungry!
MISS BENNETT:	Some pickles?
JOHN:	No, thanks.
MISS BENNETT:	A glass of milk?
JOHN:	Yes, please. I'm thirsty, too!

Communication Points
Greet and leave people

When you meet people you say:

Hello!————————————————————————————————————▶
Hi!————————————————————————————————————▶
GOOD MORNING————————————▶ GOOD AFTERNOON————▶ GOOD EVENING————▶

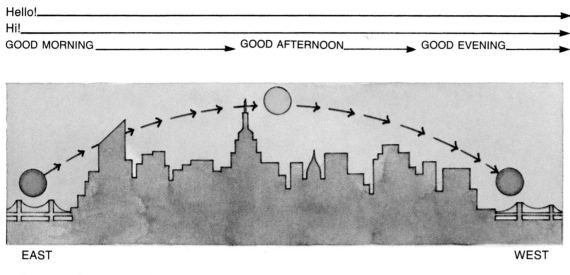

EAST   WEST

When you leave people you say:

Goodbye ————————————————————————————▶
Bye ————————————————————————————————▶
See you later/soon ————————————————————————▶
So long ——————————————————————————————▶
            See you tomorrow———▶
            Good night————————▶

Practice the dialogues with your partner. Use the information below.

TIME	YOU MEET:	YOU LEAVE:
8:30 A.M.	Mrs. Day	Bill
10:10 A.M.	Mr. Cooper	John
11:20 A.M.	Carol	Mr. Day
3:00 P.M.	Mrs. Cooper	Janet
4:15 P.M.	Miguel	Sue

TIME	YOU MEET:	YOU LEAVE:
5:20 P.M.	Miss Bennett	Tim
8:05 P.M.	Dr. Koga	your teacher
9:00 P.M.	Andrew	Carlos
10:00 P.M.	your teacher	Mrs. Koga

YOU:	Good morning, Mrs. Day.
MRS. DAY:	Good morning!
YOU:	What time is it, please?
MRS. DAY:	It's 8:30.
YOU:	Thank you.

TIM:	What's the time, . . . ?
YOU:	It's 5:20.
TIM:	Oh, it's late! Bye . . . !
YOU:	Bye! See you tomorrow.

Locate people and rooms

1. Practice dialogues like this.

> A: Hey, Janet?
> B: Yes?
> A: Where are you?
> B: Here—in the kitchen.

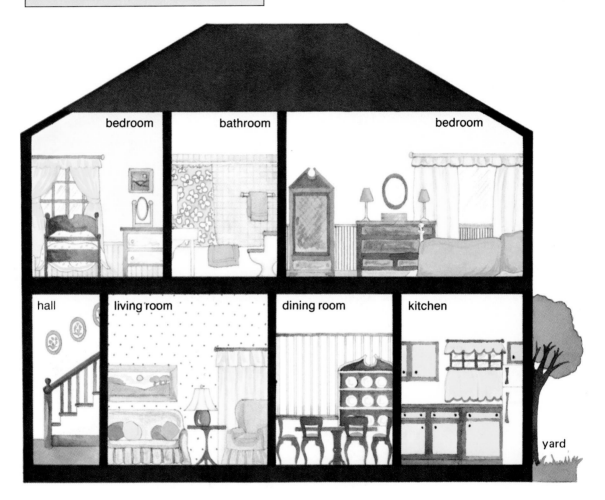

2. Play hide-and-seek. Hide in the house. Your partner will try to find you.

> A: Are you in the bedroom?
> B: Yes, I am./No, I'm not.

3. Draw a house. Hide Bill, Carol, John, Janet, Miguel, and Tim in the rooms or in the yard. Your partner will try to find them.

> A: Is Tim in the hall?
> B: Yes, he is./No, he isn't.

4. Ask your partner to name each of the rooms. Then change roles.

> A: What's room *a*?
> B: It's the living room.

a.
c.
e.
b.
d.

Offer something

Your partner offers you something to eat or drink. Say: *Yes, please* or *No, thanks* (or *No, thank you*).

> A: Have a glass of milk?   A: Some pickles?
> B: No, thanks.   B: No, thank you.
> A: A sandwich?
> B: Yes, please.

glass of milk   apple   cup of tea   cup of coffee

cup of hot chocolate   banana   pear   cookies   pickles

can of grape soda   glass of lemonade   glass of orange juice   bowl of ice cream

slice of cake   piece of apple pie   grapes   slice of bread   bowl of soup

Language Points

Reading

How to make Tim's grilled cheese sandwiches

You need:

bread

cheese

a frying pan

butter

Instructions

1. Put a piece of butter into the frying pan.

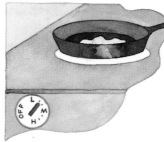

2. Melt the butter over low heat.

3. Cut a slice of cheese.

4. Put the cheese on a slice of bread. Put another slice of bread on top.

5. Put the bread and cheese in the pan. Cover the pan.

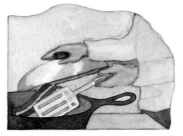

6. Wait till the bottom is brown. Check to make sure.

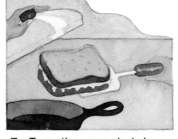

7. Turn the sandwich over. Cover the pan again.

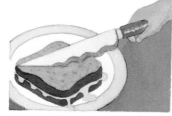

8. Put the sandwich on a plate. Cut it in half, and eat it!

a. **Read the instructions. Find four or more words that tell things you do when you make Tim's cheese sandwiches. (Each of these words is the first word of a sentence.) Now make one new sentence with each of these words.**

b. **Close your book and tell how to make grilled cheese sandwiches.**

Listening

Tim, John, Carol, and Janet are in a coffee shop. On your paper, write what they drink and what they eat.

	Tim	John	Carol	Janet
DRINK	???	???	???	???
EAT	???	???	???	???

Sing a song!

GOOD PICKLES

If you have some good pick - les and give your neigh - bor
chocolate cook - ies
grilled cheese sandwiches

none, Then you can't have an - y of my good pick - les when
chocolate cook - ies
grilled cheese sandwiches

your good pick - les are gone. CHORUS: Oh, won't it be
chocolate cook - ies
grilled cheese sandwiches

joy - ful, joy ful, joy - ful, Oh, won't it be

joy - ful when your good pick - les are gone.
chocolate cook - ies
grilled cheese sandwiches

Practice Points

1. **Write sentences. Use a question mark for your questions and a period for your answers.**

   Tim/kitchen. *Where's Tim? He's in the kitchen.*

   Now write sentences with these words.

   Carol/yard; Bill/bathroom; Mr. and Mrs. Cooper/yard; Pedro/kitchen; Miguel/dining room; Carlos/bedroom; Sue/hall; Dr. and Mrs. Koga/ dining room; John/bathroom.

2. **Offer things to eat and drink. Write twelve (or more) sentences.**

3. **Close the book and write the instructions for making grilled cheese sandwiches.**

4. **One day, John tries to make Tim's grilled cheese sandwiches for Mr. and Mrs. Cooper. He forgets to put the butter in the pan. What happens? Why does it happen?**

Check Points

Communication Points

Greet and leave people	Good afternoon. See you tomorrow.
Locate people and rooms	Where are you?/Here, in the kitchen.
Offer something	Have a grilled cheese sandwich.

Where are you?	Here, in the	kitchen. bedroom.

Is	Tim Carol	in the	kitchen? bedroom?

Have	an	apple.
	a	banana. bowl of soup. can of soda. cup of tea. glass of milk. piece of apple pie. slice of cake.
	some	cookies.

Words and Expressions

apple	coffee	hall	of	some
banana	cookies	heat	orange juice	soup
bathroom	cover	hot chocolate	pear	tea
bedroom	cup	hungry	pickles	teacher
bottom	cut	ice cream	pie	thirsty
bowl	dining room	kitchen	piece	top
bread	eat	lemonade	plate	turn
butter	frying pan	living room	put	wait
cake	glass	low	sandwich	yard
check	grapes	melt	slice	
cheese	grilled	milk	soda	

Good afternoon.   See you later.
Good evening.   See you soon.
Good night.   See you tomorrow.
No, thanks.   Yes, please.

cookies   biscuits

WHERE DO YOU LIVE?

CAROL: Mom, Janet and I go to the same school.

MRS. DAY: Oh, really? What grade are you in, Janet? Are you in Carol's class?

JANET: Yes. We're in the same class.

MRS. DAY: How nice. And where do you live?

JANET: Well, I'm from San Francisco, but now I live here, in Riverdale.

MRS. DAY: I see. And what about your family?

JANET: Well, we all live in New York. My father's a doctor at Fordham Hospital.

MRS. DAY: And your mother?

JANET: She's a computer programmer. And I have two brothers, Kenji and Andrew.

MRS. DAY: Two brothers? How old are they?

JANET: Kenji's fifteen and Andrew's eighteen. And I have a sister, Patricia. You know her, Carol.

CAROL: Oh, yes. She's nineteen.

MRS. DAY: You have a big family, don't you?

JANET: Yes, I do!

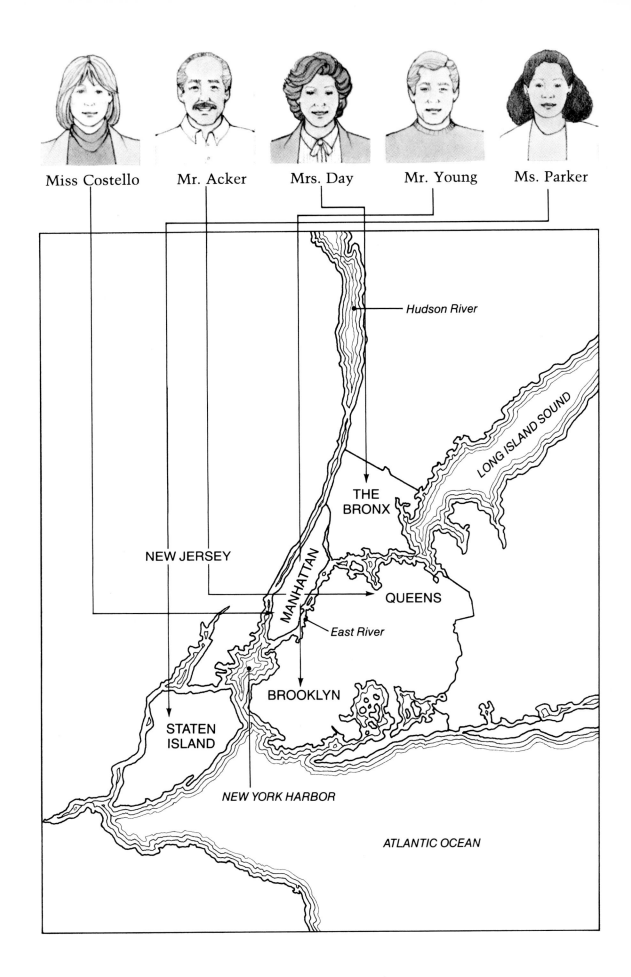

Miss Costello   Mr. Acker   Mrs. Day   Mr. Young   Ms. Parker

Hudson River

LONG ISLAND SOUND

THE BRONX

NEW JERSEY

MANHATTAN

QUEENS

East River

STATEN ISLAND

BROOKLYN

NEW YORK HARBOR

ATLANTIC OCEAN

Communication Points

Find out where people live

1. **Look at the people and the map on page 68 and find out what part of New York they live in. Then ask and answer with your partner like this:**

> A: Where do you live, Miss Costello?
> B: I live in Manhattan.

2. **Ask your partner where he/she lives.**

3. **Practice these dialogues with your partner.**

> MRS. DAY: Where do you live, Janet?
> JANET: I'm from San Francisco, but I live in New York now.
> MRS. DAY: What about your family?
> JANET: We all live in New York.

> MRS. DAY: Where do you live, Tim?
> TIM: I'm from London, but I live in New York now.
> MRS. DAY: What about your family?
> TIM: They live in London.

4. **Practice the dialogues again. This time play the roles of Mrs. Day talking to Pedro, Sue, Gina, and Carlos. Use the information below.**

> Pedro is from Mexico City. He is in New York now, but his family is in Mexico City.

> Sue is from Toronto. She is in New York now, but her family is in Toronto.

> Gina is from Naples, but she and her family live in New York now.

> Carlos is from Acapulco, but he and his family live in New York now.

Talk about family

THE KOGA FAMILY TREE

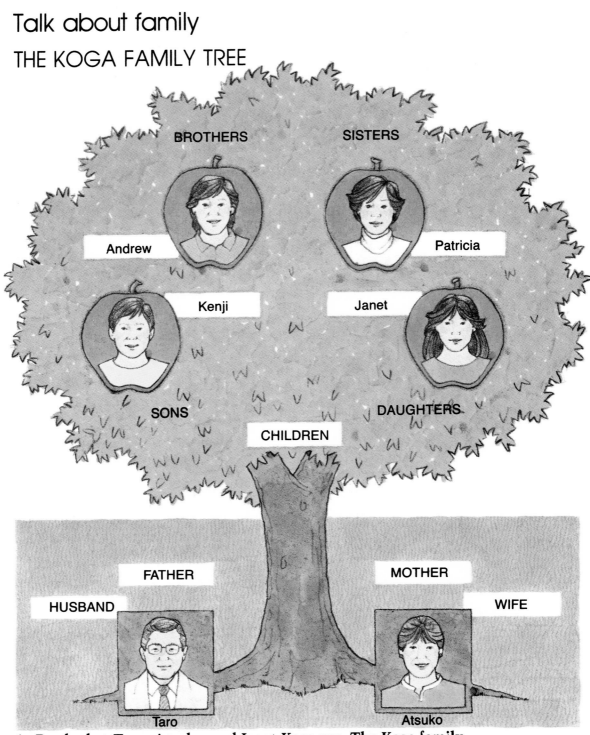

1. Read what Taro, Atsuko, and Janet Koga say. The Koga family tree will help you to understand.

TARO: I'm Taro Koga. This is my wife, Atsuko. I have four children: two sons, Kenji and Andrew, and two daughters, Patricia and Janet.

ATSUKO: I'm Atsuko Koga. This is my husband, Taro. I have four children: two sons, Kenji and Andrew, and two daughters, Patricia and Janet.

JANET: I'm Janet Koga. This is my father, Taro Koga, and my mother, Atsuko. I have one sister, Patricia, and two brothers, Kenji and Andrew.

2. **On your paper, complete what Patricia, Kenji, and Andrew say about their family. Then read it aloud to your partner.**

PATRICIA: I'm Patricia Koga. This is my father, . . . , and this is my mother, ... I have one sister, . . . , and two brothers, . . . and . . . .

KENJI: I'm Kenji Koga. This is my . . . , . . . , and this is my . . . , ... I have one . . . , . . . , and two . . . , Patricia and . . . .

ANDREW: I'm . . .   . This is . . . . . . , . . . , and this is . . .   . I have . . .   . . . , . . . , and . . .   . . . , . . . and . . . .

3. **Draw the Cooper family tree and the Day family tree on your paper. Fill in the labels.**

The Coopers   The Days

??? — John   ??? — Bill   ??? — Carol
                          ??? — Bill   ??? — Carol

?? — Walter Cooper   ?? — Brenda Cooper   ?? — Jim Day   ?? — June Day

4. **Play the role of each member of the Cooper and the Day families. Describe your family like this:**

I'm . . . .   This is . . . .   I have . . . .

Identify people's jobs

| Mr. Cooper | Mrs. Cooper | Mr. Day | Mrs. Day |
| photographer | teacher | lawyer | engineer |

| Mr. Koga | Mrs. Koga | Carlos | Barbara |
| doctor | computer programmer | reporter | student |

A: Mr. Cooper's a photographer.
B: What about Mrs. Cooper?
A: She's a teacher.

Language Points

Ask and write

1. **Find out where your classmates come from and where they live. Put your information on charts like these.**

Where They Come From	
Cities or Countries	Number of Students

Where They Live	
Cities or Countries	Number of Students

2. **Now write a report like this:**

Our school is in . . .
Ten students are from Mexico.
Six students are from . . .
Two students are from . . .

Find their jobs

Find out these people's jobs and write them on your paper.

a. I'm a ecetahr.

b. I'm a reuocpmt ermagrprmo.

c. I'm a rocodt.

d. I'm a prterreo.

e. I'm a reyawl.

f. I'm a tetunsd.

g. I'm an negneier.

h. I'm a repratohpogh.

Listening

Listen to the radio program. Write the people's jobs on your paper.
Make two charts like these:

The Browns	
Mr. Brown	???
Mrs. Brown	???
Bill	???
Joan	???

The Walkers	
Mr. Walker	???
Mrs. Walker	???
Philip	???

Memory game

Look at the picture for two minutes, then close the book and write all the things you can remember.

Practice Points

1. **Complete these sentences on a piece of paper.**

    a. Where . . . you live, Janet? . . .   . . . in New York.
    b. . . .   . . . from New York? No, ... from San Francisco.
    c. . . .   . . . your family? . . . all . . . in New York.
    d. Where . . . John and Tim live? . . .   . . . in New York, too.
    e. . . . Paris in England? No, ... in France.
    f. . . . you English, Tim? Yes, ... But I live in New York.
    g. And what . . . your family? . . .   . . . in London.
    h. My family and I . . . from Acapulco, but . . .   . . . in Mexico City.

2. **Write sentences like these:**

    Carol is in the kitchen. Janet is in the kitchen.
    Carol and Janet are in the kitchen.

    Mr. Cooper is a photographer. Mr. Smith is a photographer.
    Mr. Cooper and Mr. Smith are photographers.

    a. Mrs. Cooper is a teacher. Mrs. Smith is a teacher.
    b. Tim is at the football game. John is at the football game.
    c. Pedro is at the stadium. Miguel is at the stadium.
    d. Mrs. Day is an engineer. Mr. Brown is an engineer.
    e. Mr. Day is a lawyer. Miss Brown is a lawyer.
    f. Taro Koga is a doctor. Jim White is a doctor.
    g. Bill is in the dining room. His mother is in the dining room.
    h. Carlos is a reporter. Miss Davis is a reporter.

Check Points
Communication Points

Find out where people live

Where do you live?
I'm from San Francisco, but I live in New York now.
What about your family?
They all live in New York.

Talk about family

I have one sister, Janet, and
two brothers, Kenji and Andrew.

Identify people's jobs

Mr. Cooper's a photographer.

Where	do	you they	live?

I'm We're You're	from	San Francisco, London, Tokyo,	but	I we you	live in	New York Mexico City Chicago	now.

| I have | one | brother. sister. |
| | two three | brothers. sisters. |

| Mr. Cooper Mr. Day | is | a photographer. |
| | | an engineer. |

| What about | Mrs. | Cooper? Day? |
| | Barbara? | |

Words and Expressions

all	do	lawyer	sister
brother	doctor	live	son
children	engineer	photographer	wife
class	family	reporter	
computer programmer	hospital	same	
daughter	husband	school	

How nice.
I see.

What about . . . ?
Yes, I do.

11 WHAT ABOUT A PICNIC?

JANET: Tomorrow's Saturday, isn't it?

CAROL: Yes, it is.

JANET: I have an idea. What about a picnic?

CAROL: A picnic? Where?

BILL: Well, let's go to Pelham Bay Park.

JANET: Pelham Bay? Hmmm. It's too far.

BILL: Well, let's go to Central Park. We can go by subway.

CAROL: Okay. I'll call Tim and John.

JANET: Good idea. And give me a call tonight. Do you have my phone number?

CAROL: No, I don't.

JANET: Well, it's 616-9239.

CAROL: 616-9239. Okay. Bye, Janet.

JANET: Bye, you guys! I'll see you tomorrow.

BILL: So long! Take care!

Communication Points
Name and spell the days of the week

1. Repeat the names of the days of the week after your teacher.

Sunday   Monday   Tuesday   Wednesday   Thursday   Friday   Saturday

2. Ask and answer with your partner.

> A: How do you spell
>   Wednesday?
> B: W-E-D-N-E-S-D-A-Y

Give suggestions

Key to Activities

1. Mon. Wed. Fri.
   a concert
   Central Park
   Flushing Meadows Park
   Prospect Park

2. Sat. Sun.
   a football game
   Inwood Hill Park
   Prospect Park
   Pelham Bay Park

3. Thurs. Sat. Sun.
   a bike ride
   Central Park
   Riverside Park
   Pelham Bay Park

4. Wed. Sat. Sun.
   a tennis match
   Silver Lake Park
   Riverside Park
   Bronx Park

5. Thurs. Sat. Sun.
   a picnic
   Van Cortlandt Park
   Bronx Park
   Flushing Meadows Park

6. Mon. Tues. Fri.
   a soccer game
   Central Park
   Prospect Park
   Van Cortlandt Park

Read the "Key to Activities," and suggest what to do. Your partner will suggest where to go. Then change roles.

> A: Today (tomorrow) is Sunday.
>   What about a picnic?
> B: Okay. Let's go to Central Park.

Tell what people do

1. **Read the following sentences.**

He lives in New York City.
He works for *News Events* magazine.
He speaks French.
He plays the piano.
He reads detective stories.
He likes rock music.

She lives in San Francisco.
She works for the North-West Company.
She speaks Portuguese.
She plays the guitar.
She reads music magazines.
She likes classical music.

2. **Play this game with your partner. Tell your partner one sentence about one of these people. Your partner will try to find out who you are talking about. Use more sentences until your partner guesses the person. Then change roles.**

> A: This person lives in New York City.
> B: Carmen?
> A: No. This person plays the piano.

a. Anton
City: New York City.
Employer: *News Events* magazine.
Language: French
Instrument played: piano
Favorite books: detective stories
Favorite music: rock music

b. Carmen
City: New York City
Employer: *News Events* magazine
Language: French
Instrument played: piano
Favorite books: detective stories
Favorite music: classical music

c. Helga
City: San Francisco
Employer: *News Events* magazine
Language: French
Instrument played: piano
Favorite books: detective stories
Favorite music: rock music

d. David
City: New York City
Employer: *News Events* magazine
Language: Portuguese
Instrument played: piano
Favorite books: detective stories
Favorite music: rock music

e. Paula
City: New York City
Employer: *News Events* magazine
Language: French
Instrument played: guitar
Favorite books: detective stories
Favorite music: rock music

f. José
City: New York City
Employer: *News Events* magazine
Language: French
Instrument played: piano
Favorite books: novels
Favorite music: rock music

Ask what people have

**1. Look at the list. What things do you have? Write the names of the
things you have.**

Do you have . . .

a telephone	a guitar	a football	a bird
a car	a cassette recorder	a truck	a cat
a bike	a radio	a clock	a dog
a watch	a TV set	a motorcycle	a typewriter
a pen	a record player	a sister	
a piano	a camera	a brother	

2. **Ask your partner what things he or she has. Write the names of the things your partner has.**

> A: Do you have a telephone?
> B: Yes, I do./No, I don't.

Language Points

Letter writing

1. **Here's a letter from Roberto, a Brazilian boy, to John. Roberto received John's name and address from a pen pal club.**

Rua Cultoa Sciencia, 397
Rio de Janeiro, Brazil
18 March, 1986

Dear John:
   My name is Roberto Arantes. I am thirteen and I am in the first year of junior high school. I am Brazilian, and I live in Rio de Janeiro, but I come from São Paulo. I have two brothers, Arturo and José, and one sister, Manuela. Arturo is fourteen, José is nine, and Manuela is four.
   My father works for a rubber company here, and my mother is a teacher. I have a white cat, Socrates, and a yellow bird. Do you have a pet?
   Write soon.
           Yours,
           Roberto
           Here's my photo

2. **Read Roberto's letter. Then write your own letter in English to a pen pal in another country. Be sure to start every sentence with a capital letter and end it with a period.**

Listening

Listen to find out when the people go, what they do, and where they go. Make a chart like this to write your answers.

Day of the Week	What the People Do	Where the People Go
Dialogue 1 ????	????	????
Dialogue 2 ????	????	????
Dialogue 3 ????	????	????

Role play

You	Your Partner
a. Ask your partner where he/she lives.	b. Say where you live.
c. Say what day of the week it is tomorrow. Suggest a place to go.	d. Say that the place is too far away.
e. Suggest another place.	f. Accept. Ask your partner to call you tonight.
g. Ask your partner his/her telephone number.	h. Say your telephone number.
i. Thank your partner and say goodbye	

Practice Points

1. Can you find the days of the week? Write the words on your paper.

a. ADDENSEWY b. DIRAFY c. UNDYAS d. YADSTURA
e. SYATEDU f. NYDOAM g. HARSUTYD

2. Write dialogues. Use page 77 for help.

> A: Today is Sunday. What about a picnic?
> B: Okay. Let's go to Central Park.

Central Park

Fountain, Central Park

Delacorte Theatre, Central Park

Central Park Lake

Seal Harbor, Coney Island

The Cloisters, Fort Tryon Park

3. Look at the pictures and look at the list of sentences. Choose the sentences that tell about each person. Write them on your paper under the person's name. Notice capital letters and copy correctly.

a. Andy

News Events *magazine—Dallas*

b. Ann

North West Company—San Francisco.

c. Mrs. Cooper

Brown School—Chicago

d. Dr. Koga

Fordham Hospital—New York.

He lives in New York.
He likes rock music.
He plays the piano.
She reads music magazines.
He likes classical music.
She speaks Portuguese.
She likes classical music.
He works for Fordham Hospital.
She speaks French.
She likes rock music.
She plays the piano.
He lives in Dallas.

He speaks French
She plays the guitar.
He reads detective stories.
She lives in Chicago.
He speaks French.
She works for the North West Company.
He plays the piano.
He reads detective stories.
He works for *News Events* magazine.
She lives in San Francisco.
She reads detective stories.
She works for the Brown School.

4. Read this paragraph about Andy.

Andy lives in Dallas, Texas, and works for *News Events* magazine. He speaks French and plays the piano. Andy reads detective stories and likes rock music.

Now write about Ann, Mrs. Cooper, and Dr. Koga in the same way.

Check Points

Communication Points

Name and spell days of the week	How do you spell Wednesday? W-E-D-N-E-S-D-A-Y
Give suggestions	What about a picnic? Let's go to Central Park.
Tell what people do	She/he lives in New York City/ works for *News Events magazine* speaks French/plays the piano/ reads detective stories/likes rock/ classical music
Ask what people have	Do you have a telephone? Yes, I do./No, I don't.

What about a	picnic? tennis match?	Let's go to	Central Park. Bronx Park.

He She	lives in New York City. speaks Portuguese. works for *News Events* magazine. reads detective stories. plays the guitar. likes rock music.

Do you have	my phone number? a telephone?	Yes,	I	do.
		No,		don't.

Words and Expressions

bird	dog	magazine	soccer	work
cat	far	park	tennis match	
classical music	give	piano	today	
clock	idea	picnic	tonight	
concert	letter	ride	typewriter	
detective stories	like	rock music	week	

Days of the Week
Sunday   Thursday
Monday   Friday
Tuesday   Saturday
Wednesday

Bye, you guys!
Take care!

A PICNIC WITH MUSIC 12

CAROL: Let's go down near the lake. We can hear the music from there. There are lots of people here tonight!

TIM: This is a good place, isn't it?

BILL: Yes, it is. Janet, do you have the chicken sandwiches?

JANET: No, I don't. Carol has them. Come on, Carol, pass the sandwiches!

TIM: Here's some lemonade.

JANET: Oh, look! There's the first band! What is it? What's its name, I mean.

TIM: I don't know.

BILL: The Fat Cats. Let's listen!

CAROL: They're fantastic! I really like their music. It's something else!

TIM: Hey look, there's the lead singer!

BILL: I'm hungry. Let's have the sandwiches.

CAROL: Oh, Bill! Let's listen.

Communication Points
Ask and say what people have

chicken sandwiches

apples

bread

water

eggs

bananas

cola

cheese sandwiches

butter

lemonade

chicken sandwiches
water

cola
apples
eggs

lemonade
cheese sandwiches

bread
bananas
butter

1. **Look at the pictures and complete the following sentences on your paper.**
   a. Carol has the chicken sandwiches and . . . .
   b. Tim has . . . and . . . and . . . .
   c. Bill . . . .
   d. Janet . . . .

2. **Ask and answer.**

> A: Does Carol have the chicken sandwiches?
> B: Yes, she does.

> A: Does Carol have the eggs?
> B: No, she doesn't.

Talk about yourself

1. Answer the questions on your paper. Write *Yes* or *No* for each question.

Do you speak
a. Spanish?
b. English?
c. Japanese?

Do you play
j. the piano?
k. the guitar?
l. the drums?

Do you like
d. rock music?
e. jazz?
f. classical music?

Do you eat
m. spaghetti?
n. rice?
o. Mexican food?

Do you read
g. comics?
h. science fiction?
i. newspapers?

Do you drink
p. cola?
q. orange juice?
r. coffee?

2. Now ask your partner the questions.

> A: Do you speak Spanish?
> B: Yes, I do./No, I don't.

Describe pictures

1. Look at picture a on the following page for about two minutes. Then describe the picture to your partner. Use the sentences below. Your partner will look at the picture and check whether you are right or wrong. Then reverse roles for picture b.

a. There is a phone booth in the picture.
b. There are two phone booths in the picture.
c. There is a watch in the poster.
d. There is a glass in the poster.
e. There is a bus in the street.
f. There are two buses in the street.
g. There are three watches in the shop window.
h. There are four glasses in the shop window.
i. There is a woman at the bus stop.
j. There are two women at the bus stop.
k. There is a boy on a bicycle.
l. There are two boys on bicycles.
m. There is a pony in the street.
n. There are three ponies in the street.

a.

b.

2. Choose one of the four pictures, c, d, e, or f. Your partner will try to guess your picture.

| A: | Is there a bus? |
| B: | Yes, there is./No, there isn't. |

| A: | Are there two buses? |
| B: | Yes, there are./No, there aren't. |

c.

d.

e.

f.

Language Points
Reading

Central Park Lake

NEW YORK PARKS

New York has many, many parks, and there is always something going on in them. There are concerts in Central Park, Prospect Park, Flushing Meadows, and other parks. Rock groups, bands, symphony orchestras, and famous singers such as Barbra Streisand perform in the parks. In the outdoor theater in Central Park, actors put on plays. Thousands of New Yorkers come to watch and listen.

People play in the parks, too. They play baseball, football, and tennis. They ride bikes and horses. They row boats. In some parks, they swim. Coney Island and Rockaway Park have beaches on the Atlantic Ocean. On hot days, the beaches are crowded with people swimming and enjoying the sun.

Many of the parks in New York are quite large. But New York has small parks, too. In Washington Square Park, artists show their new paintings. In Battery Park, New York's oldest park, people look at the harbor or line up to take the ferry boats to Staten Island or the Statue of Liberty. Other boats take people from Battery Park on a trip around Manhattan Island.

There is something for everybody in New York's parks. Do you like animals? There are several zoos in different parts of the city. Do you like ice skating? You can skate outdoors in winter and indoors all year. Do you like to run or jog or hike? There are lots of places for this. And you can have a picnic almost anywhere.

If you go to New York, be sure to see the parks. You can hear your favorite music. You can play your favorite games. Or you can just sit, rest, and watch the people. Whatever you choose, you'll enjoy it.

Read "New York Parks." Then complete these sentences on your paper. A blank (. . .) can be one word or several words.

a. There is always . . . in New York parks.

b. Rock groups and famous singers . . . .

c. Actors . . . in Central Park.

d. People ride . . . in the parks.

e. You can even find beaches . . . .

g. Many parks in New York are quite large, but Washington Square Park is . . . .

g. The oldest park in New York is . . . .

h. A boat trip around Manhattan Island leaves from . . . .

i. For people who like animals . . . .

A concert in Central Park

Bronx Park Zoo

Riverside Park

Bronx Park Botanical Garden

Central Park

Flushing Meadows - Corona Park

Listening

1. **Listen to the dialogue and write on your paper what Rosa, Mike, and Jimmy have for their picnic. Make a chart like this.**

Rosa	Mike	Jimmy

2. **Copy the questions on page 86 on your paper. Then listen to Bill's interview and write his answers.**

Practice Points

1. **Copy the following sentences on your paper and complete them. Use *have* or *has.***

   a. Tim . . . the bananas.

   b. Bill . . . the cola.

   c. Janet and Patricia . . . two brothers.

   d. Mr. and Mrs. Bennett . . . three children.

   e. I . . . a red bike.

   f. My father . . . a new truck.

   g. We . . . a radio and a TV.

   h. Carol . . . a small camera.

   i. John . . . a nice watch.

   j. I . . . a cassette recorder.

2. **Look at the pictures on page 85 and answer these questions on your paper. Notice the comma in the answers.**

Does Carol have the chicken sandwiches?	Yes, she does.
Does Tim have the butter?	No, he doesn't.

   a. Does Janet have the eggs?

   b. Does Bill have the apples?

   c. Does Tim have the cola?

   d. Does Bill have the eggs?

   e. Does Carol have the water?

   f. Does Tim have the cheese sandwiches?

   g. Does Carol have the bread?

   h. Does Janet have the lemonade?

3. **Read this chart.**

	Pincushion	The Music Makers	The Fat Cats
Drums			✓
Organ	✓		
Singer	✓		✓
Trumpet		✓	✓
Piano		✓	✓
Guitars	✓	✓	

4. **Look at the chart on page 90. Write ten sentences about the groups.**

> Pincushion has an organ, but it doesn't have a piano.
> The Music Makers and the Fat Cats have trumpets, but they don't have organs.

5. **Complete the following sentences on your paper. Use your answers to the questions on page 86.**
   a. I speak . . . , but I do not speak . . . .
   b. I read . . . , but I do not read . . . .
   c. I like . . . , but I do not . . . .
   d. I play . . . , but . . . .
   e. I eat . . . , but . . . .
   f. I drink . . . , but . . . .

6. **Write all the questions you have to ask to do exercise 2 on page 87.**

7. **Write descriptions of the four pictures in exercise 2 on page 87. Use complete sentences.**

8. a. **Read the dialogues in Units 2, 3, 4, 5, 6, 7, 10, 11, and 12. Write all the sentences in these dialogues that use *my, your, his, her, its, our, their.***
   b. **Underline *my, your, his, her, its, our, their.***
   c. **Write the names of the people or things that these words refer to.**

   (Unit 2) What's your name? (Carol)

Check Points
Communication Points

Ask and say what people have	Carol has the chicken sandwiches and Tim has the cheese sandwiches. Does Carol/Tim have the chicken sandwiches? Yes, she/he does./No, she/he doesn't.
Talk about yourself	Do you eat rice? Yes, I do./No, I don't.
Describe pictures	There is a phone booth. There are two buses in the street.

I You We They	have	the chicken sandwiches.
He She	has	

Do	I you we they	have the eggs?
Does	he she	

Yes,	I you we they	do.
	he she	does

No,	you I we they	don't.
	he she	doesn't.

There	is	a phone booth in the park. a bus on the street.
	are	two buses. two boys.

Is	there	a bus? a boy?
Are		two buses? two boys?

Yes,	there	is. are.
No,		isn't. aren't.

What's	my your his her its our their	name?

one car	two cars
one sandwich	two sandwiches
one bus	two buses
one box	two boxes
one boy	two boys
one baby	two babies

Words and Expressions

bicycle	eggs	organ	shop	water
chicken	fantastic	pass	spaghetti	window
Chinese	food	picture	Spanish	woman
cola	good	pony	their	
comics	jazz	rice	them	
drums	lake	singer	trumpet	

Come on.   It's something else.
Hey, look!   lots of . . .
I mean . . . .

DO YOU LIKE PETS? 13

CAROL:	Look at that dog! Isn't it beautiful?
TIM:	Yes, it is. It looks like an Afghan.
CAROL:	Really? Do you like dogs, Tim?
TIM:	Well, not very much, in fact.
BILL:	Don't you like pets, Tim?
TIM:	Yes, but I prefer cats.
JANET:	So do I. And I like birds, too.
CAROL:	I don't. I think they're stupid.
TIM:	Stupid? I don't think so. I have a parrot at home in England.
BILL:	You do? Does he talk?
TIM:	No, he doesn't. He's too young. He's only 40 years old.

Communication Points
Ask and talk about likes and dislikes

1. Ask and answer.

A: Do you like dogs?	A: Do you like cats?
B: Yes, I do.	B: No, I don't.

Pets

dogs   cats   parrots   goldfish

hamsters   turtles   canaries

2. Look at the pictures and find out which pets Bill and Carol like and don't like.

BILL

LIKES   DISLIKES

CAROL

LIKES   DISLIKES

3. Ask and answer.

| A: Does Bill like . . . ? | A: Does Carol like . . . ? |
| B: Yes he does./No, he doesn't. | B: Yes, she does./No, she doesn't. |

4. Say which pets Bill and Carol like and don't like.

Bill likes . . . .   He doesn't like . . . .

Agree and disagree

MOVIES	MUSIC	DRINKS	DESSERTS
Romantic stories	Rock	Milk	Cheesecake
Detective stories	Pop	Tea	Chocolate cake
Cartoons	Disco	Coffee	Apple pie
Science fiction	Folk	Hot chocolate	Doughnuts
Horror films	Jazz	Cola	Yogurt
Westerns	Classical	Lemonade	Ice cream
Comedies	Country and Western	Apple juice	Fruit

1. **What do you prefer in each of the columns, MOVIES, MUSIC, DRINKS, and DESSERTS? Write your choices on your paper.**

2. **Ask your partner what he or she likes, and say if you agree or disagree.**

> A: What kind of movies do you like?
> B: I like horror films.
> A: So do I. / I don't. I prefer westerns.

3. **Ask about your classmates' likes and dislikes. Use the chart above. Write the answers on your paper and make a report to your partner.**

Name and spell months

1. Repeat the names of the months after your teacher.

2. Ask and answer.

> A: How do you spell January?
> B: J-A-N-U-A-R-Y

3. Name the missing months.

> A: January, February . . . ?
> B: March

Language Points
Reading and writing

1. Read the letter from Tim to his sister Betty.

> 28 Jones Street
> New York, N.Y. 10014
>
> April 22
>
> Dear Betty,
>   I'm writing to tell you that I have a new friend.
> His name's Bill Day. He's 14 and is very nice.
>   He lives in Brooklyn Heights with his family, but
> he goes to my school. He has a sister, Carol, and she goes
> to our school, too. She's 13 and is very nice. Their father's
> a lawyer, and their mother's an engineer.
>   After school, Bill and I often go to the park.
> We play baseball and watch people walking their
> pets. People walk all kinds of dogs there, and some
> people even take their cats for walks.
>   Some days Bill and I listen to music. He likes
> rock, but he doesn't like jazz. That's a pity, but
> anyway we have a very good time together. I miss
> London, but   I ♡ 🍎
>   Do you know what that means? I love "the Big Apple."
> That's what people call New York.
>   I must hurry now. I'm meeting Bill at four o'clock.
> Write soon.
>   Love,
>   Tim

2. Now write a letter to one of your friends. Tell him or her about another friend. Tell what this person likes and dislikes and what you do together. Be sure to indent the first line of each paragraph in your letter.

Practice Points

1. Reread the dialogue, "Do You Like Pets." Then write short answers to the questions on page 99.

| Are Janet, Bill, and Carol in Bronx Park? | No, they aren't. |
| Do they see an Afghan? | Yes, they do. |

a. Does Tim like dogs?
b. Does Tim like pets?
c. Does Tim prefer cats?
d. Does Janet prefer cats?
e. Does Janet like birds, too?
f. Does Carol like birds?
g. Does Tim have a bird at home?
h. Is it a parrot?
i. Does he talk?
j. Is he old?

2. **Write these months of the year.**
   a. a month with three letters
   b. two months with four letters
   c. two months with five letters
   d. a month with six letters
   e. two months with seven letters
   f. three months with eight letters
   g. a month with nine letters

3. **Look at the examples.**

   I like coffee. *I don't. I prefer tea.*

   I'm a teacher. *I'm not. I'm a student.*

   I like dogs. *So do I.*

   I'm a student. *So am I.*

   Now you do the same. Tell about yourself in your answers.

   a. I live in New York.
   b. I like rock music.
   c. I speak English.
   d. I play football.
   e. I'm fifteen.
   f. I like horror films.
   g. I'm from San Francisco.
   h. I play the guitar.
   i. I like cheesecake.
   j. I like cats.

Check Points
Communication Points

Name and spell months	How do you spell January? J-A-N-U-A-R-Y
Ask and talk about likes and dislikes	Do you like dogs? Yes, I do./No I don't. Does Bill like cats? Yes, he does./No, he doesn't.
Agree and disagree	I like dogs. So do I. I don't. I prefer cats.

Do	you				Yes,	I	do.		No,	I	don't
		like	dogs? cats? birds?			he she	does.			he she	doesn't.
Does	Bill Carol										

I like	dogs. cats. birds.	Bill Carol Tim	doesn't like	cats. dogs. birds.	So do I./I don't. I prefer	birds. hamsters. canaries.

Words and Expressions

			Names of Months	
Afghan	goldfish	science fiction	January	July
beautiful	hamster	see	February	August
canaries	horror films	stories	March	September
cartoons	kind	stupid	April	October
cheesecake	month	talk	May	November
comedies	only	think	June	December
country	parrot	turtles		
disco	pets	western		
doughnuts	pop music	yogurt		
folk music	prefer			
fruit	romantic			

I don't think so.   in fact   That's a pity.
I must hurry now.   looks like   You do?

Sing a song!

OLD MACDONALD

1. Old Mac-Don-ald had a farm, E - I - E - I - O! And on this farm he had some *Chicks E - I - E - I - O! With a *chick chick here, and a chick chick there, Here a chick, there a chick, ev-'ry-where a chick chick, Old Mac-Don-ald had a farm, E - I - E - I - O!

*2. Dog   Woof Woof   5. Cow   Moo Moo
 3. Cat   Meow Meow   6. Donkey   Hee Haw
 4. Sheep Baa Baa

WHY DON'T WE HAVE A HAMBURGER?

BARBARA: Gee, I'm tired today.

CARLOS: You are? Well, I'm hungry. Let's go to "La Fondue."

BARBARA: What's that?

CARLOS: It's a French restaurant on West 51st Street. Maurice works there.

BARBARA: Maurice? Who's Maurice? What does he do?

CARLOS: He's a friend of mine. He's a waiter.

BARBARA: Hmmm. French restaurants are expensive. And I'm broke! Why don't we have a hamburger instead?

CARLOS: Great idea! I'm thirsty, too. Let's get two hamburgers and a couple of root beers.

CARLOS: Two hamburgers, please.

WAITER: How do you want them?

BARBARA: One rare . . .

CARLOS: . . . and one well done.

WAITER: That's $1.90.

CARLOS: And two root beers, please.

WAITER: Two root beers. Here you are.

CARLOS: How much is it all together?

WAITER: That's $2.80.

CARLOS: $2.80? That's cheap enough, isn't it?

Communication Points
Identify people and their jobs

1. Read the sentences.

Maurice is a waiter.
Ricardo is a mechanic.
Shoji is a photographer.
Garth is a dancer.

Carlo is a builder.
Bill is an editor.
Patty is a golfer.
Nan is a police officer.

Carmen is a pilot.
Annette is a chef.
Allison is a farmer.
Elly is a painter.

2. Match the sentences with the pictures.

a.

b.

c.

d.

e.

f.

g.

h.

i.

j.

k.

l.

3. Point to each picture and ask:

A: Who's that?
B: It's Nan.
A: What does she do?
B: She's a police officer.

Give suggestions

a. sandwich
b. hot dog
c. cola
d. root beer
e. lemonade
f. hamburger
g. taco
h. pizza

1. Practice making suggestions with your partner like this:

> A: I'm hungry.
> B: Why don't you have a hamburger?

> A: I'm thirsty.
> B: Why don't you have a root beer?

2. Ask and answer.

> A: I'm hungry, why don't we have a hamburger?
> B: Good idea. I'm thirsty, too. Let's have two hamburgers and a couple of root beers.

Suggest alternatives

1. Look at these activities.

play baseball	go to a restaurant	stay at home
go to the movies	play cards	have a hamburger
go for a bike ride	watch TV	listen to records

2. Make suggestions for the activities. Your partner will make different suggestions. Then change roles.

> A: Let's . . . .
> B: Oh, I'm tired./I'm broke. Why don't we . . . instead?

Ask and say prices

American Money: Bills

ONE DOLLAR $1

FIVE DOLLARS $5

TEN DOLLARS $10

TWENTY DOLLARS $20

Coins

one cent	five cents	ten cents	twenty-five cents	fifty cents	$1 1.00
1¢ .01	5¢ .05	10¢ .10	25¢ .25	50¢ .50	a dollar
a penny	a nickel	a dime	a quarter	a half dollar	

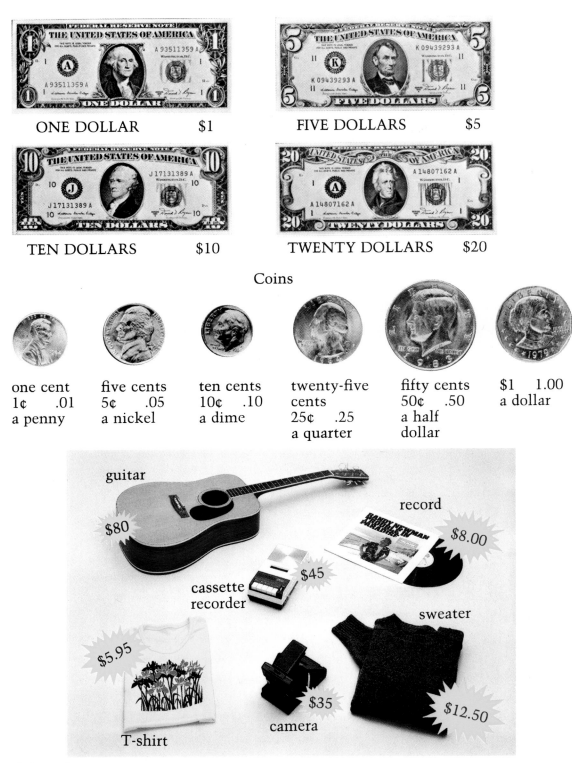

guitar $80

record $8.00

cassette recorder $45

sweater $12.50

$5.95

T-shirt

camera $35

Ask and answer:

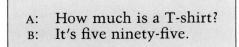

A: How much is a T-shirt?
B: It's five ninety-five.

Language Points

Check prices

Mrs. Koga and Janet went shopping yesterday. Look at the prices in the pictures and check the cash register receipts. Are there any mistakes?

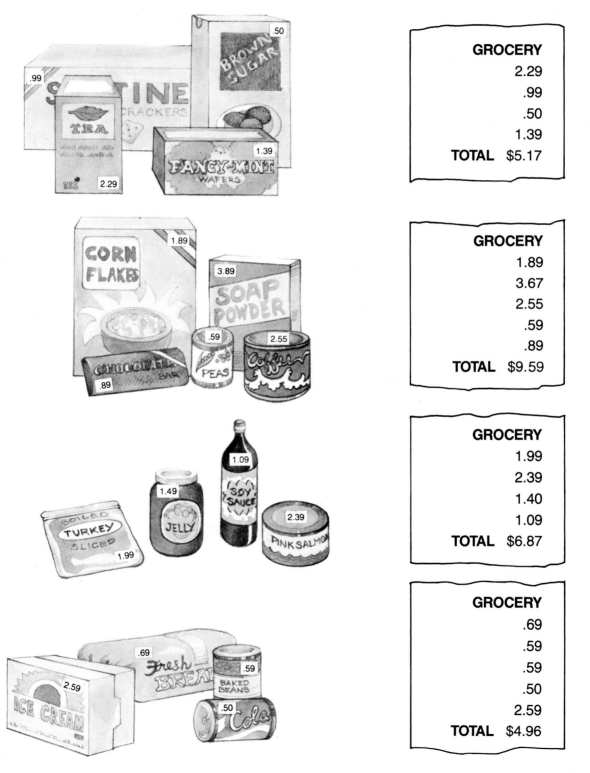

GROCERY	
	2.29
	.99
	.50
	1.39
TOTAL	**$5.17**

GROCERY	
	1.89
	3.67
	2.55
	.59
	.89
TOTAL	**$9.59**

GROCERY	
	1.99
	2.39
	1.40
	1.09
TOTAL	**$6.87**

GROCERY	
	.69
	.59
	.59
	.50
	2.59
TOTAL	**$4.96**

Role play

Coffee House Menu

DRINKS

Coffee . . . . 30¢   Hot Chocolate . . . . 35¢

Tea . . . . 30¢   Orange Juice . . . . 45¢

Milk Shakes . . . . 50¢   Cola . . . . 45¢

GRILLED SANDWICHES

Ham and Cheese . . . . 65¢   Cheese and Tomato . . . . 50¢

SOUP

Tomato Soup . . . . 45¢

Soup of the Day . . . . 45¢

Hot Dog . . . . 75¢

SPECIALTIES

Spaghetti Plate . . . . 99¢

Pizza $3.50

Hamburger . . . . 95¢

DESSERTS

Apple Pie . . . . 50¢   Coffee Cake . . . . 45¢

Danish Pastry . . . . 60¢   Cheesecake . . . . 65¢

Order from this menu for yourself and two friends. Your partner is the waiter and will write down your order and tell you the total price. Then change roles.

| A: | A coffee, two orange juices and three cheesecakes, please. | B: | That's $3.15 all together. |

Listening

Listen to the conversation. On your paper write the prices of the portable television, the radio, and the guitar.

Guess the price

Guess the prices of the objects. The person who comes nearest to the real prices is the winner.

Role play

YOU	YOUR PARTNER
a. Tell your partner you're hungry. Suggest having a pizza.	b. Answer that you're hungry, too, but that you're broke. Ask how much a pizza is.
c. Say a pizza costs $3.50.	d. Say it is too expensive. Suggest having a hamburger.
e. Say it's good idea. Order two hamburgers.	

Practice Points

1. **This is a picture of Bill's family. Ask Bill who each person is. Write your questions and Bill's answers on your paper. Follow the punctuation in the example.**

> *Who's that?*
> *It's my sister, Carol.*

2. **Draw a picture of your family. Ask and answer questions the same way. Write your questions and answers.**

3. **Look at the pictures on page 102 and write a short dialogue about each of the characters.**

> A: What does Nan do?
> B: She's a police officer.

4. **Copy and complete the following dialogue. Use *I'm hungry, I'm thirsty, I'm tired,* or *I'm broke.***

    a. A: . . . . Let's get a hot dog.
        B: . . . too. Let's have two hot dogs and a couple of root beers.
    b. A: . . . . Let's stay at home and watch TV.
        B: Good idea! I'm tired, too.
    c. A: . . . . Let's have a cola.
        B: And. . . . Let's get two sandwiches, too.
    d. A: Tomorrow's Saturday. Let's go to the movies.
        B: No,. . . . Let's go for a bike ride instead.

5. Copy and complete. Use: *have a cola, have a lemonade, have a hamburger, have a pizza, watch TV, play cards,* **or** *stay at home.*

> A: I'm thirsty. What about you?
> B: I'm thirsty, too. Why don't we have a lemonade?

a. A: We're hungry.
   B: . . . ?
b. A: Let's go to the movies.
   B: I'm broke. What about you?
   A: I'm broke, too. . . . ?
c. A: Let's play baseball.
   B: Hmmm. I'm tired. . . . ?
d. A: I'm hungry.
   B: . . . ?
e. A: Let's go for a walk. Are you tired?
   B: Yes, I am. . . . ?
f. A: Bill and I are thirsty.
   B: . . . ?

6. Write the following prices in words.

35¢	40¢	$2.05	$4.25	95¢
$30	$2.01	$10	5¢	

Check Points

Communication Points

Identify people and their jobs	Who's that?
	It's Maurice.
	He's a waiter.
Give suggestions	Why don't you have a hamburger?
	Why don't we have a sandwich?
Suggest alternatives	Let's play baseball.
	No, I'm tired. Why don't we play cards instead?
Ask and say prices	How much is a T-shirt?
	It's five ninety-five.

Who's that?	It's	Maurice. Nan. Bill.

What does	he she	do?

He's She's	a	waiter. farmer.
	an	editor.

I'm	hungry. thirsty.

Why don't	you we	have a	hamburger? sandwich? cola? lemonade?

Let's	play baseball. watch TV. go to the movies.

How much is a	T-shirt? guitar? record?

Words and Expressions

builder	editor	menu	pizza	tired
cards	expensive	milkshakes	police officer	tomato
cent	farmer	nickel	restaurant	T-shirt
cheap	golfer	painter	root beer	waiter
dancer	hamburger	pastry	stay	who
dime	hot dogs	penny	sweater	
dollar	mechanic	pilot	taco	

a couple of	Here you are.	Let's go/get . . . .
a friend of mine	How much is it all together?	watch TV
Gee, ...	I'm broke.	Why don't we . . . instead?
Great idea!		

bill
(money)

note

Sing a song!

KUM BA YA

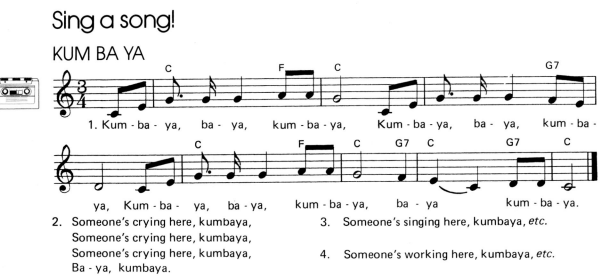

1. Kum - ba - ya, ba - ya, kum - ba - ya, Kum - ba - ya, ba - ya, kum - ba - ya, Kum - ba - ya, ba - ya, kum - ba - ya, ba - ya kum - ba - ya.

2. Someone's crying here, kumbaya,
   Someone's crying here, kumbaya,
   Someone's crying here, kumbaya,
   Ba - ya, kumbaya.

3. Someone's singing here, kumbaya, *etc.*

4. Someone's working here, kumbaya, *etc.*

5. Someone's sleeping here, kumbaya, *etc.*

DO YOU WANT TO GO TO THE MOVIES? 15

MISS BENNETT:	Can you answer that, Tim?
TIM:	Of course. Hello.
BILL:	Hi, Tim. This is Bill.
TIM:	Hello, Bill.
BILL:	What are you doing, Tim? Right now, I mean.
TIM:	Nothing special. I'm reading a magazine.
BILL:	Do you want to go to the movies with Carol and me?
TIM:	Sure—great idea! What's playing?
BILL:	*Murder on the Orient Express.* It's a mystery.
TIM:	Okay. What time does it start?
BILL:	At five.
TIM:	Five o'clock? Which theater?
BILL:	The ABC. Do you know where it is?
TIM:	Wait a minute. Isn't it on Bleecker Street?
BILL:	No, that's the Circle. The ABC is on University Place, near Union Square.
TIM:	University Place?
BILL:	Never mind, Tim. We'll come and pick you up at your house.
TIM:	Thanks, that'll help. Is a quarter to five okay?
BILL:	That's fine. See you at quarter to five.
TIM:	Goodbye.
BILL:	Bye!

Communication Points
Identify actions

a.   b.   c.   d.   e.   f.   g.

1. **Each of these sentences goes with one of the seven pictures. Decide which sentence goes with each picture and write it on your paper with the letter of the picture.**

     f. *Martina Navratilova is playing tennis.*

Stevie Wonder is singing.
Liza Minnelli is dancing.
Martina Navratilova is playing tennis.
Yoko Ono is playing the piano.

Scott Hamilton is skating.
Sally Ride is piloting a space shuttle.
The Incredible Hulk is growling.

2. **Look at the pictures again. Ask and answer like this:**

> A: What's Stevie Wonder doing?
> B: He's singing.

Invite people
Accept or refuse invitations

1. Which of these invitations would you like to receive? Make a list.

Do you want to	Do you want to
a. go to the movies tonight?	f. help me with my homework?
b. come to a party?	g. go on a picnic?
c. go to a rock concert?	h. do the dishes?
d. play tennis?	i. play baseball?
e. go for a walk tomorrow?	j. play soccer?

2. Talk to your partner. Ask and answer like this.

> A: Do you want to go to the movies tonight?
> B: Sure—great idea!/No, thanks. It's too late.

> A: Does your brother want to go to the movies tonight?
> B: No. He has to do his homework.

If you refuse the invitation, give a reason. Look at these examples.

> I'm doing my homework./I have to go to my guitar lesson.
> It's my birthday today./I'm tired./It's too late.

Ask and give information.

Look at the *New York Amusement Guide* on page 114. Choose the show(s) you would like to see, and invite your partner. Ask and answer like this.

> A: Do you want to go to the movies?
> B: Hmm. What's playing?
> A: A mystery. It's at the ABC.
> B: A mystery? Great! What time does the show start?
> A: At five.
> B: Where's the theater?
> A: It's on University Place.

ABC 5:00 University Place 7:30 10:00 **Murder on the Orient Express** A mystery by Agatha Christie	BELASCO TUES-SAT 8:00 W. 45th St. WED & SAT 3:00 SUN 3:00, 7:00 **The Merchant of Venice** A comedy by W. Shakespeare
72nd Street Playhouse WEEK & SUNDAY between 1st 2:00-5:10-8:20 & 2nd Ave. **The FRISCO KID** A great Western	MAJESTIC TUES-SAT 8:00 245 W. 44 St. WED & SAT 2:00 SUN 3:00 **THE MOUSETRAP** A mystery by Agatha Christie
THALIA SAT. & SUN. 5:15-8:00 Broadway at 95th WEEK 4:30 **"FRANKENSTEIN'S RETURN"** The classic horror film	CARNEGIE HALL SUNDAY, AUGUST 10 W. 57th St. at 8 p.m. **Dave Brubeck and his Quartet** Jazz concert

Tell a story

With your partner, put these sentences in order so that they tell a story. Then draw a picture to go with each sentence and write the sentence under the picture. Be careful! Be sure that the sentences are in the correct sequence.

1. Now Dr. Koga is in the restaurant, and he is drinking a cup of coffee.
2. Dr. Koga is running out of the restaurant, but it is too late; the police officer is writing out a ticket.
3. Dr. Koga is parking his car on Lorillard Place.
4. A police officer is coming down the street.
5. He is going into the Fordham Coffee House, his favorite restaurant, but his car is in a "no parking" zone.
6. Dr. Koga is watching the baseball game on TV.

Language Points
Listening

Listen to the dialogues. On your paper write which people accept the invitation to go to the movie, and write the kind of movie it is. Make a chart like this.

Person	Accept?	Name of Movie	Kind of Movie
John	????	*The Frisco Kid*	????
Tim	????	*Dracula*	????
Janet	????	*Murder on the Nile*	????

Practice Points

1. **Copy the following sentences and complete them. Use *am, is,* or *are,* plus the *-ing* form of the word in parentheses. The first one is done for you.**

   a. Dr. Koga . . . his car. (park) *Dr. Koga is parking his car.*
   b. I . . . . (eat)
   c. John and Tim . . . tennis. (play)
   d. Carol . . . milk (drink)
   e. Miss Bennett is . . . TV. (watch)
   f. Bill and Janet . . . to the movies. (go)
   g. They . . . at the disco. (dance)
   h. We . . . in the park. (skate)

2. **Read the dialogue on page 113 ("Ask and give information") and write five similar dialogues. Use the information in the *New York Amusement Guide*.**

Check Points
Communication Points

Identify actions	Stevie Wonder is singing.
Invite people	Do you/Does he want to go to the movies?
Accept or refuse invitations	Sure—great idea! No, thanks, It's too late./I have to go to my guitar lesson./He has to do his homework.
Ask and give information	What's playing? A mystery. It's at the ABC./It's at five./It's on University Place.
Tell a story	Dr. Koga is parking his car.

What	am	I		doing?		I	am		skating.
	are	you we they				You We They	are		reading a magazine. playing tennis. eating.
	is	he she it				He She It	is		

Do you Does he	want to	to go the movies? play tennis? come to a party?		No,	thanks, I have to	go to my guitar lesson.
					he has to	do his homework.

Words and Expressions

answer	homework	skate	do the dishes	of course
dance	invitation	start	Never mind.	right now
down	mystery	theater	Nothing special.	What are you doing?
favorite	out	which		
growl	park (car)	write		
help	run			

mystery	thriller
theater	theatre
favorite	favourite

Sing a song!

I JUST CALLED

Words and Music by
STEVIE WONDER

1. No New Year's Day to celebrate;
   no choc'late covered candy hearts to give away.
   No first of spring; no song to sing.
   In fact here's just another ordinary day.

2. No April rain; no flowers bloom;
   no wedding Saturday within the month of June.
   But what it is, is something true,
   made up of these three words that I must say to you.

3. No summer's high; no warm July;
   No harvest moon to light one tender August night.
   No autumn breeze; no falling leaves;
   Not even time for birds to fly to southern skies.

4. No Libra sun; no Halloween;
   No giving thanks to all the Christmas joy you bring.
   But what it is, though old so new
   To fill your heart like no three words could ever do.

(to Chorus:)

CHORUS: I just called to say I love you.
   I just called to say how much I care.
   I just called to say I love you.
   And I mean it from the bottom of my heart.

WHAT DID YOU DO LAST NIGHT?

ALBERT FINNEY
INGRID BERGMAN
SEAN CONNERY

Murder on the Orient Express

NOW SHOWING
ABC THEATER

JOHN: Good game, wasn't it?

TIM: Yes, it was! But I'm a little tired.

JOHN: You need to play more often, Tim.

TIM: You're right.

JOHN: Hey, did you go to the movies last night?

TIM: Yes, I did.

JOHN: What did you see?

TIM: I saw *Murder on the Orient Express*.

JOHN: What kind of movie is it?

TIM: It's a mystery. It's about the little fat detective with the bow tie and bowler hat.

JOHN: Oh, Hercule Poirot. How was the movie?

TIM: It's an old film . . . but it was good.

JOHN: Did you go alone?

TIM: No, Carol and Bill were there, too. How about you? Did you go anywhere?

JOHN: No, I didn't. I stayed at home. I watched TV all evening.

Communication Points

Ask and tell about past actions
WHAT DID YOU DO YESTERDAY?

 1. stayed at home

 2. went to school

 3. went to the movies

4. went for a bike ride

 5. watched TV

6. went swimming

 7. got up early

 8. got up late

 9. played tennis

10. played baseball

 11. went to bed early

 12. went to bed late

1. Make a chart like this and write what you did yesterday.

	YESTERDAY	
Morning	Afternoon	Evening/Night

2. Ask your partner questions from the following chart.

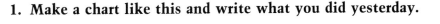

Did you	stay at home go to school go to the movies go for a walk go swimming watch TV	get up early get up late play tennis play baseball go to bed early go to bed late	yesterday	morning? afternoon? evening?
What else did you do			last night?	

> A: Did you stay at home last night?
> B: Yes, I did. / No, I didn't. I went to the movies.

Ask and tell where people were

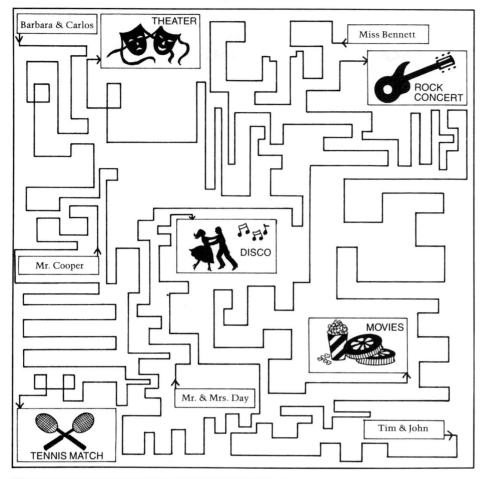

Barbara & Carlos — THEATER
Miss Bennett — ROCK CONCERT
Mr. Cooper
DISCO
MOVIES
Mr. & Mrs. Day
Tim & John
TENNIS MATCH

A: Where was Miss Bennett last night?
B: She was at the . . . .

A: Where were Barbara and Carlos last night?
B: They were at the . . . .

Ask and tell what people looked like

Talk about the people in the pictures.

A: Was King Henry fat or thin?
B: He was fat.

A: Was Napoleon tall or short?
B: He was short.

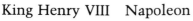

King Henry VIII   Napoleon   Abe Lincoln   Queen Victoria   President Taft

Language Points

Listening

Listen to the dialogues and write on your paper what the people did last night.

Reading

1. **Newspapers and magazines often have reviews of concerts, movies, plays, and books. Read this review of *Murder on the Orient Express*.**

ALBERT FINNEY IS POIROT IN 1974 CHRISTIE MYSTERY

Murder on the Orient Express, the 1974 movie from Agatha Christie's famous mystery story, is now playing at the ABC Theater.

The cast includes Albert Finney, Sean Connery, and Richard Widmark. There is an Academy Award performance by Ingrid Bergman.

Finney stars as Hercule Poirot, the Belgian detective. As the film starts, many well-dressed passengers are boarding the famous Orient Express train. Among them is the small and rather fat detective, Poirot, with his bowler hat and bow tie.

During the night, a bad snowstorm stops the train in the mountains. One of the passengers is murdered. Detective Poirot tries to find out who is the murderer.

The end of the movie shows Poirot talking to all the passengers. He brilliantly solves the difficult case, as he curls the ends of his mustache upward.

Agatha Christie, author of *Murder on the Orient Express,* is one of the most famous mystery writers of the twentieth century. More than 400 million copies of her books were sold during her lifetime. She was the author of more than 80 novels. The well-dressed and elegant Hercule Poirot is the hero of many of them. Agatha Christie was born in England in 1890 and died there in 1976.

2. **What did Hercule Poirot look like? From each box, choose the picture that fits the description of Poirot in the review.**

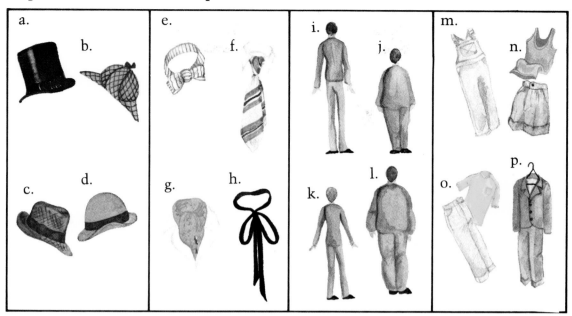

3. **Ask and answer with your partner.**

> A: Did Poirot wear a tie like this?
> B: Yes, he did./No, he didn't.

Practice Points

1. **Write questions to go with these answers. Be sure to start each question with a capital letter and end it with a question mark.**

   a. Yes, I did. The movie was very good.
   b. Mr. Cooper? He was at the tennis match.
   c. No, I didn't. It was Sunday, so I got up late.
   d. Barbara and Carlos? They were at the disco.
   e. Oh, Yes. I stayed at home all day.
   f. Miss Bennett? She was at the movies.
   g. No, I didn't. I went to bed at 11 o'clock last night.
   h. Mr. and Mrs. Day? They were at the theater.
   i. Yes, I went for a bike ride in Central Park.
   j. No, I didn't. Schools are closed on Saturdays.

2. **Copy and complete the paragraph. Use the correct forms of the words in the box. You can use each word more than once.**

   Yesterday Tim .⁽ᵃ⁾. late. It .⁽ᵇ⁾. Sunday morning so he .⁽ᶜ⁾. in bed until 10 o'clock. At eleven he .⁽ᵈ⁾. to Van Cortlandt Park with Bill and John. They .⁽ᵉ⁾. baseball for a couple of hours. At the end, they .⁽ᶠ⁾. a little tired, so they sat on a bench and had an ice cream cone. In the afternoon, Tim and John .⁽ᵍ⁾. to the movies: there was an old John Wayne western at the Odeon theater, and they had a lot of fun. In the evening, Tim had supper with Miss Bennett and then he .⁽ʰ⁾. TV. There .⁽ⁱ⁾. a mystery on, but Tim .⁽ʲ⁾. very tired, so he .⁽ᵏ⁾. to bed early.

be
get up
go
play
stay
watch

Check Points

Communication Points

Ask and tell about past actions	What did you do yesterday?
	Did you stay at home?
	Yes, I did./No, I didn't.
	I went to school.
Ask and tell where people were	Where was Miss Bennett last night?
	She was at the . . .
	Where were Barbara and Chris?
	They were at the . . .
Ask and tell what people looked like	Was King Henry fat or thin? He was thin.

Did you	stay at home? go to school? get up early? watch TV? play tennis?

Yes, I did.	
No, I didn't, I	stayed at home. went to school. got up late. watched TV. played baseball.

Where	was were	Miss Bennett Barbara and Carlos	last night?

He She	was	at the	movies. disco. tennis match. theater.
They	were		

Was	King Henry Abe Lincoln Queen Victoria	fat or thin? tall or short?	He She	was	fat. thin. tall. short.

Words and Expressions

afternoon	evening	old	was
alone	fat	played	watched
anywhere	film	saw	wear
bed	get up	short	went
bench	got up	stayed	were
clothes	hat	supper	yesterday
did	night	tall	
early	often	thin	

all evening   How about you?   What else . . . ?
a lot of fun   I'm a little . . . .   You're right.

Words and Expressions

Number words, color names, and similar grouped words follow the expressions at the end of this list. Numbers refer to the units in which words and expressions are introduced.

a	1	cartoons	13	engineer	10	home run	6	nationality	3
add	4	cassette		English	1	homework	15	near	8
address	7	recorder	1	evening	16	horror films	13	newspaper	7
Afghan	13	cat	11	expensive	14	hospital	10	nickel	14
afternoon	16	cent	14	family	10	hot chocolate	9	night	16
again	7	cheap	14	fans	6	hot dogs	14	no	3
airplane	5	check	9	fantastic	12	hungry	9	not	3
all	10	cheese	9	far	11	husband	10	now	4
alone	6	cheesecake	13	farmer	14	I	2	o'clock	4
alphabet	8	chicken	12	fat	16	ice cream	9	of	9
American	1	children	10	father	3	idea	11	often	16
an	5	Chinese	12	favorite	15	I'm (I am)	2	old	16
and	3	city	3	film	16	in	3	on	3
answer	15	class	10	fine	8	invitation	15	only	13
anywhere	16	classical		folk music	13	is	1	orange juice	9
am	2	music	11	food	12	it	4	organ	12
apple	9	clock	4	football	1	Italian	5	our	5
are	2	clothes	16	football field	8	Japanese	3	out	16
art	7	club	7	football game	4	jazz	12	painter	14
at	4	coffee	9	for	1	kind	13	park	11
ball	6	cola	12	friends	3	kitchen	9	park (a car)	15
banana	9	color	5	from	2	know	10	parrot	13
baseball	6	comedies	13	fruit	13	lake	12	pass	12
basketball	7	comics	12	frying pan	9	last name	7	past	7
bat	6	computer		German	5	late	5	pastry	14
bathroom	9	programmer	10	get up	16	lawyer	10	pear	9
batter	6	concert	11	give	11	lemonade	9	pen	1
be	6	cookies	9	glass	9	lesson	7	penny	14
beautiful	13	country	13	go	6	letter	11	pets	13
bed	16	cover	9	goldfish	13	library	6	phone booth	8
bedroom	9	cup	9	golfer	14	like	11	phone number	7
bench	16	cut	9	good	12	listen	12	photographer	10
bicycle	12	Dad	3	got up	16	live	10	piano	11
big	5	dance	15	grapes	9	living room	4	pickles	9
bike	5	dancer	14	great	6	look	5	picnic	11
bird	11	daughter	10	grilled	9	low	9	picture	12
book	1	detective		growl	16	magazine	11	pie	9
bottom	9	stories	11	guitar	7	mechanic	14	piece	9
bowl	9	diamond	6	half	7	meet	3	pilot	14
bread	9	did	16	hall	9	meeting	7	pizza	14
brother	10	dime	14	hamburger	14	melt	9	plate	9
builder	14	dining room	9	hamster	13	menu	14	play	6
bus	5	disco	13	hat	16	Mexican	1	played	16
bus stop	4	do	10	have	6	milk	9	police officer	14
but	5	doctor	10	he	2	milkshakes	14	pony	12
butter	9	dog	11	heat	9	Miss	3	pop music	13
cake	9	dollar	14	help	15	month	13	post office	6
camera	1	doughnuts	13	her	4	mother	3	poster	1
can	6	down	15	here	3	motorcycle	5	prefer	13
Canadian	2	drink	6	here's (here is)	1	movies	4	present	1
canaries	13	drums	12	he's (he is)	1	Mr.	3	put	9
can't	6	early	16	him	8	Mrs.	3	quarter	7
car	5	eat	9	his	4	my	2	radio	1
card	7	editor	14	hit	6	mystery	15	read	6
cards	14	eggs	12	home	8	name	2	ready	4

record	7	skate	15	talk	13	tonight	11	were	16
record player	1	slice	9	tall	16	too	5	western	13
restaurant	14	small	5	tea	9	top	9	what's (what is)	2
reporter	10	so	6	teacher	9	train	5	where	2
rice	12	soccer	11	team	6	truck	5	which	15
ride	11	soda	9	tennis match	11	trumpet	12	who	14
road	7	some	9	telephone	7	T-shirt	14	wife	10
rock music	11	something	6	that	5	turn	9	window	12
romantic	13	son	10	the	3	turtles	13	with	4
room	4	soup	9	theater	15	TV	1	woman	12
root beer	14	spaghetti	12	their	12	typewriter	11	work	11
run	16	Spanish	12	them	12	up	6	write	16
same	10	speak	8	there	5	very	8	yard	9
sandwich	9	spell	8	they	4	visit	3	yes	2
saw	16	start	15	thin	16	wait	9	yesterday	16
school	7	stay	14	think	13	waiter	14	yogurt	13
science	7	stayed	16	thirsty	9	was	16	you	1
science fiction	13	stories	13	this	1	watch	1	young	6
see	13	street	7	throw	6	watched	16	your	2
she	2	student	7	time	4	water	12	you're (you are)	2
she's (she is)	1	stupid	13	tired	14	we	4	zoo	4
shop	12	subway station	8	to	3	wear	16		
short	16	supper	16	today	11	week	11		
singer	12	sweater	14	tomato	14	well	8		
sister	10	taco	14	tomorrow	7	went	16		

Expressions

a couple of	14	How old are you?	6	See you tomorrow.	9
a friend of mine	14	Hurry up!	4	so long	8
all evening	16	I don't know.	5	strike out	6
all right	6	I don't think so.	13	Take care!	11
a lot of fun	16	I'm a little ...	16	thanks	1
as usual	5	I'm broke.	14	Thank you.	1
At last!	5	I mean ...	12	That's a pity.	13
Bye!	4	I must hurry now.	13	That's right.	5
Bye, you guys!	11	I'm not too young ...	6	They're something else!	12
Come in.	1	in fact	13	watch TV	14
Come on!	12	I see.	10	What about ...?	10
do the dishes	15	Keep your eye on the ball.	6	What are you doing?	15
Excuse me.	7	Let's go.	4	What else?	16
Gee....	14	Let's go/get ...	14	What time is it?	4
Good afternoon.	9	Let's go look at it.	5	Well, ...	3
Goodbye.	4	Look at him go!	6	Why don't we ... instead?	
Good evening.	9	looks like	13	Wow!	5
Good morning.	4	lots of	12	Yes, I do.	10
Good night.	9	never mind	15	Yes, please.	9
Great idea!	14	Nice to meet you.	3	You do?	13
Happy birthday!	1	No, thanks.	9	You're right.	16
Have a good time!	3	Nothing special.	15	You're up!	6
Hello!	1	of course	15	You're welcome.	1
Here you are.	14	Oh, gosh!	4		
Hey, look!	12	Oh, I see.	3	**Number Names**	
Hey, you guys!	5	Oh, really?	3	1–12	4
Hi!	1	Oh, sure.	7	13–23	6
Hold on a minute.	8	Oh, thanks.	1	30–90	7
How about you?	16	Okay	7		
How are you?	8	over there	5	**Color Names**	5
How do you do?	3	Please	7	black pink orange	
How much?	4	right now	15	blue red	
How much is it		See you...	8	brown white	
all together?	14	See you later.	9	green yellow	
How nice.	10	See you soon.	9	Days	11
				Months	13